# THE
# HAPPINESS
# HANDB☺☺K

# THE
# HAPPINESS
# HANDB☺☺K

simple ways to

change your

life for the better

LISA T.E. SONNE

FALL RIVER PRESS

New York

## FALL RIVER PRESS

New York

An Imprint of Sterling Publishing
1166 Avenue of the Americas
New York, NY 10036

Cover design by David Ter-Avanesyan
Book design by Kevin Ullrich

ISBN 978-1-4351-6122-1

For information about custom editions, special sales, and premium
and corporate purchases, please contact Sterling Special Sales at
800-805-5489 or specialsales@sterlingpublishing.com.

Manufactured in the United States of America

2  4  6  8  10  9  7  5  3  1

www.sterlingpublishing.com

# Prelude

LIFE IS FULL OF POSSIBILITIES FOR RADIANT JOY, ENDURING love, deep contentment, belly-shaking laughter, satisfying success, soaring bliss, sweet smiles, excellent wins, best friends, astonishing pleasure, quiet peace, and rewarding purpose. It can also suck.

Happiness is what you make of life. It's a choice, a way, a process, not a destination, product, or quota.

Most of us already know the basics:

Love well.

Laugh well.

Eat well, sleep well, move well, give well for well-being.

Be good, do good, think good thoughts for a good life.

There can be a big gap, though, between words and ideas on the one hand, and actual experiences and reality on the other. Most of us could use some help with momentum and motivation, and some insights to guide our choices. How about some wisdom from other civilizations and some gems from big research engines?

To help inspire, here's a sampler of definitions, quotes, activities, tools, examples, and research about happiness. There are diverse bits from Aristotle, Einstein, Ryan Seacrest, Groucho Marx, a teenager, Buddha, Jesus, Stanford and Harvard universities, the United Nations, and maybe even the kitchen sink.

These happy messages are intended to help you truly enjoy and fulfill your life. We need allies for joy. In the United States alone, billions of dollars are spent manipulating fears and insecurities to get you to *spend money and buy stuff*—supposedly to make your life better and happier.

What most people really want, however, is to spend *time* well and to *enjoy* stuff that may already be within them or within their reach—the "stuff" being people and purposes more than products.

We need to overcome the consumer messages that permeate and bombard our worlds, so we can hear our own messages—the ones we choose and use. Most of us also have internal negative monologues that don't serve us, and those can also be weighted with external social expectations that aren't consistent with our true aims.

As if all that wasn't hard enough, we approach our desire to "be happy" with an evolutionary disadvantage. Harkening back to caveman days, humans are wired to have the brain receive messages of fear more quickly than messages of joy. Survival dictated that "avoiding pain" trumps "seeking pleasure." Of the commonly recognized human facial emotions—fear, anger, surprise, sadness, contempt, disgust, and joy—only one is overtly positive.

Today, in the twenty-first century, scientists and researchers say unhappiness from the "negativity bias" of human wiring can be overcome with new habits, intentions, and choices. They are also finding that individual "happiness" has its basis in genetic and environmental circumstance, in addition to the powerful influences of our individual behavior and mindset.

The following pages can help you change the factors under your control. They are a mix of happiness suggestions for both the short- and long-term. You'll find ways to boost your mood for an instant pickup, tips to evolve your outlook, habits for a higher daily baseline of happiness, and paths for a more pervasive sense of eternal happiness.

More than the shiny consumer goods in catalogs and ads, most of us would really like more love, health, nature, culture, playtime, contribution, meaning—these are the elements of a happy life. Interestingly, research indicates that if we focus on obtaining a combination of those elements, rather than aim for "happiness" directly, we are more likely to be happy.

Research also suggests that focusing our efforts on helping others be happier is more likely to make us happy than if we only focus on our own happiness. When we spend our money on good causes, we are happier. And research indicates that our laughs and smiles and happiness can be contagious to a degree, helping others around us be happier.

The implications of all this are amazing for you. You may never be famous or wealthy. But in the process of becoming happy, your daily sphere of influence could be powerful and positive, making the *world* happier.

*The Happiness Handbook* has a starter group of messages for you to adopt, debate, or toss. What is obvious to you may be life-changing for someone else. Ancient sages and nascent research can contradict or confirm. Start on any page, skip around, write in the margins. Add your own profundity or humor. Make this book *your* book.

There are basic ingredients for happiness, but each of us has different tastes, recipes, needs, and seasonings. Finding the right combinations can be part of our pleasures, if we set aside expectations. Think of this book as an eclectic pantry of information and "messages." Select what ingredients to cook, consume, and serve to feed you and nourish loved ones.

To your happiness!

Thanks for exploring.

—Lisa T.E. Sonne

# Eudaimonia

THE GREEK WORD *EUDAIMONIA* CAN MEAN HUMAN happiness, good welfare, or a thriving state of being. The roots of the word are *eu*, which is "happy," and *daimon*, which is "spirit." Sometimes it's spelled *eudaemonia* or *eudemonia*.

In ancient Greece, the topic of happiness was hot and hotly debated. For philosophers, it was at the core of the study of Ethics.

Aristotle believed eudaimonia was the highest human good, the ultimate aim, and it could be attained through virtue. He also recognized external influencers, like beauty, wealth, politics, and health.

The Stoic philosophers thought virtue alone was enough for eudaimonia. Virtue to ancient Greeks was not a moral judgment, but a quality and excellence. External factors weren't needed for happiness.

Other Greeks touted more sensual pleasures as the way to happiness.

The debate continues today in many languages. Are you pro-eudaimonia? Who are the happy people in your life? What's their take? When are you going to hang out with them next?

# Your Happiness

IF YOU MAKE YOUR DEFINITION FOR HAPPINESS SOMETHING that is impossible, it will be. When do you feel happiness? When do you act happy? What is possible?

*Your happiness is....*

*What if happiness is*
*Feeling the gentle sun and wind on your face?*
*Doing a kindness to someone without them knowing*
*it was from you?*
*Putting extra effort into something worthy and*
*seeing it turn out better?*
*Forgiving yourself mistakes and others, too?*
*Laughing at the absurdities of life?*
*Just being glad to be alive each day you wake up?*
*And each night you go to sleep?*
*Glad to be alive at this time and place?*
*Glad you survived—and did some savoring, too?*

*What if happiness is looking in the mirror?*
*And smiling at what is,*
*With a twinkle in each eye*
*for what has been and what can be?*

*The answers are yours.*

*Say "yes."*

*Ask the questions that matter to you.*

*Encore!*

—Olivia Muser

# Origin

THE ENGLISH WORD "HAPPY" HARKS BACK TO THE fourteenth century. It came from the Middle English noun "hap," which referred to "luck, fortune, prosperity, good chance." The words "happen" and "happenstance" come from the same root.

In Welsh, the word for "happy" originally meant "wisdom." But most European words for "happy" originally meant "luck" more than gladness or joy. One theory for the difference: The prevailing belief of the time was that one's fate was controlled by divine forces; if you were happy, you were lucky. By the late fifteenth century, there was a recorded use of "happy" meaning "very glad."

Today, happiness has a wide range of positive meanings, and many cultures believe people can influence happiness both for themselves and the social community.

# Synonyms for "Happiness"

Bliss

Cheerfulness

Contentment

Delight

Ecstasy

Elation

Enjoyment

Euphoria

Exhilaration

Exuberance

Fulfillment

Gaiety

Gladness

Glee

Felicity

Jollity

Joy

Jubilation

Lightheartedness

Merriment

Mirth

Paradise

Pleasure

Rapture

Satisfaction

Well-being

Try picking one of these synonyms and thinking about it while you brush your teeth in the morning. What memories, hopes, or songs do you conjure? Do you note any difference in your day?

Try a different word when you brush your teeth at night. Did you sleep better?

# Grooming

ACCORDING TO AN ANNUAL SURVEY BY THE U.S. BUREAU of Labor Statistics, Americans spend an average of forty minutes each day "grooming"(showering, dressing, etc.). Men average less than thirty-five minutes daily. Women spend a little more than forty-eight minutes.

That's time spent grooming in the physical sense. How much time do you spend grooming things that cannot be seen—soul, heart, mind? Can you also mentally shave off, wash away, or brush out any invisible negative debris?

While going through your morning routine, find an affirmation, chant, or some happy song lyrics. Let them run through your head as a way to gauge if you have brushed your teeth long enough.

When you see the dirty, sudsy water going down the shower drain, what fabricated fears, cancerous resentments, and unproductive anxieties can you also send down the drain? Feel all of those negativities washing away. Then put your face to the water and feel it splashed with joy.

As you soap up parts of your body, instead of thinking about your perceived physical inadequacies, can you think about how grateful you are for that part of you?

Explore how happy you can feel, spending those forty minutes grooming your beautiful self both inside and out!

# Happy Medium

To SOMEONE WHO LOVES SÉANCES, A HAPPY MEDIUM MIGHT be a person who acts as a cheerful conduit to other worlds. As an idiom, however, "happy medium" means striking the right balance and compromise between extremes.

The phrase "happy medium" first showed up in English print in the mid-eighteenth century, but the idea of middle ground goes further back as a path for a good life. In ancient Greece, Aristotle advocated "the golden mean" as the virtue (meaning "excellence" then) that can be found between the two vices or extremes of excess and deficiency. He advocated that all human actions should be motivated to aim for happiness.

In Buddhism, peace and happiness for self and others can be found by living "The Middle Way"—again, a balance between opposites, neither over-indulgence nor extreme punishment.

What are your extremes? What is your best "happy medium"?

# 100 Happy Days

"Can you be happy for one hundred days?"

That is the challenge issued by the "100 Happy Days" project, which suggests you post a photo each day of something or someone that makes you happy—from a funny sign to a baby being born. The photos are either posted privately, shared publicly, or available only to a private group that you choose. According to the project site, participants who have completed the one hundred days of photos reported several benefits:

• Noticing the pleasures in every daylife and becoming more aware of what makes them happy during routine times.

• Creating activities to photograph that could add happiness developed more "intentional happiness" in their lives.

• The joy of having a visual record to remind them that their lives looked wonderful.

• Making others happy, because people looked forward to their photos, and their "focus," through the lens and not, stimulated others to think more about happiness.

Does one hundred days sound like too much? Try starting with seven happy days. For one week, take a photo each day of something that conjures happiness.

# Good Morning!

HAPPIEST TIMES: SATURDAYS, EARLY MORNINGS, NOVEMBER, and December.

Unhappiest times: First days of the week, late nights, January.

Who says?

People's tweets, according to Cornell researchers. For two years, they examined 2.4 million tweeters from eighty-four nations. With hundreds of millions of immediate messages or micro-blog tweets crisscrossing the globe every day, Twitter is now a source of material that some behavioral scientists are mining. Researchers admit that users of Twitter may not accurately represent human populations in terms of education, income, and age. But the immediacy of the messages gives them a pulse on moods of a large population with diverse religions, backgrounds, and geographies.

This tweet analysis found that people tend to wake up feeling good, then moods drop after about two hours. On weekends this shift occurs later, probably because people sleep later. This pattern was true even for nations like Saudi Arabia, where the workweek is Sunday to Thursday.

Regardless of whether your morning tweets are from the birds or your electronic devices, how long does the good of your good mornings soar before it nosedives? Can you let the good times roll longer?

# Happiness Walks

*An early-morning walk is a blessing for the whole day.*

> —Henry David Thoreau

*In every walk with nature, one receives far more than he seeks.*

> —John Muir

STARTING YOUR DAY WALKING IN BEAUTY CAN BE AN aerobic high or a moving meditation.

Today, walking is even being called a "wonder drug," because research keeps showing that strolling and striding is good for the mind, body, and spirit.

Identified in surveys as America's favorite physical activity, walking is basically free, can be done most places and times, requires no special equipment, and is healthy and mood-enhancing for people of almost every age.

To increase the happiness benefits as you walk, you can look around and count your blessings, or listen to joyful music, or focus on your breath, or—just walk!

Whether you create a social walking club or enjoy the solitude of going solo, what happy places can you discover when you walk?

# Walk and Talks

"MEANINGFUL TALKS" ARE ANOTHER GREAT CONTRIBUTOR to happiness. Combine them with a walk through nature with a close friend, and you have a powerful happiness tool—"walk and talks."

Think of it as a combination of aerobic exercise and a supportive therapy session. Pick a wonderful local nature trail and start spilling the beans as you stride through beauty. Share the sweet and the stinky of your lives. (There's a difference between miring in the misery and detoxing emotional poisons by "airing" them out in the great fresh air.)

Sometimes the best cure is a good friend listening. A friend may also ask questions that provide a different perspective. Make sure you are also a good listener for your friend. Research shows that we feel better helping others than we do focusing on our own happiness.

By the time you reach the top of a real hill for a better vista, you may both have better views of the undulating elevations of your lives.

# Flower Power

TAKE TIME TO "SMELL THE ROSES," AND TO SEE THE petunias, daisies, or daffodils in your own home. Beauty can beat the morning blahs.

This may be a no-brainer for you, but some brains put it to the test and confirmed what you may already sense. A Harvard University and Massachusetts General Hospital study, headed by Nancy Etcoff, Ph.D., confirmed that seeing flowers in the morning can elevate your energy throughout the day.

Dr. Etcoff says that flowers can raise your compassion and decrease your anxiety, too. She also indicates that your happier state can influence others, because of a phenomenon called "mood contagion."

Why not conduct your own test? Play with flowers and try different colors, smells, and locations in your home. Then enjoy the beauty for some homegrown joy that could help others, too.

# The IT Factor

"IT" WON'T SOLVE WORLD PEACE, BUT "IT" MAY GIVE
you a piece of feeling better. "It" won't resolve our
childhood "issues," but "it" may issue a smile or two.

We each have an "it" or two, or maybe a whole bunch
of 'em. In this case, "it" is something relatively easy to do
that makes us feel happier.

"It" may be getting your car washed and seeing it
transform from smelly and grungy to a mobile sanctuary.
"It" may be dropping off some books as a donation to the
local library, and picking up a super read as long as you're
there. "It" may be chewing a favorite childhood gum.

What tickles your fancy?

Make a list of your "its" for a quickie boost of cheer.

Your "it" may be somebody else's "ick," but if "it" works
for you, use "it!"

# Happiness Survey

THE WORLD HAPPINESS REPORT COMMISSIONED BY THE United Nations, was conducted in 2012 by the Earth Institute of Columbia University, which asked people how happy they were with their lives. Here are the highlights, as reported:

- Social factors, such as the absence of corruption and the amount of personal freedom, play a greater role in happiness than income, although happier countries are often richer countries.

- Compared to thirty years ago, on average, the world has become a little happier.

- Job security and good relationships at work contribute more to job satisfaction than high pay or good hours. Unemployment ranks with bereavement and separation as a major cause of unhappiness.

- People are happier when they behave well.

- Mental health affects happiness more than any other single element that was measured, but only one-fourth of mentally ill people in advanced countries get treatment. In poorer countries, the percentage is even lower.

• Marriages that last and families that are stable contribute greatly to the happiness of both parents and children.

• Women are happier than men in advanced countries. In poorer countries, the results are mixed.

• People in middle age report the lowest level of happiness.

# Water

PLANET EARTH MAY BE BETTER NAMED PLANET WATER. About 71 percent of the surface area is water. There are five mighty oceans, more than one hundred seas, and vast networks of fresh water. Water is essential to life and has been the defining element for where human civilizations have developed. More elementally, water is why life evolved—and water can help your evolution of happiness.

Our human body is mostly water - about 60 percent overall, with the brain and heart being 73 percent and our lungs a full 83 percent water.

Even healthy people who have only a 1 percent drop in their fluid intake can feel the unhappy effects of dehydration—less ability to concentrate, less stamina, fatigue, headaches, sometimes confusion. With less water, blood in the body becomes thicker and can be up to five times harder for the heart to pump and circulate.

A simple glass of water and juicy food could make a fundamental difference in how you feel and perform. Start your day with fluids, and keep it flowing!

In this case, begin with your cup full and leave it empty so you can be filled for a happier day. Water can help you both physically and metaphysically.

Some happiness wisdom from those who sought water from Walden Pond to the seas.

*We are tied to the ocean. And when we go back
to the sea, whether it is to sail or to watch—we are
going back from whence we came.*

—John F. Kennedy

*I learned this, at least, by my experiment: that if
one advances confidently in the direction of his
dreams, and endeavors to live the life which he has
imagined, he will meet with a success unexpected
in common hours.*

—Henry David Thoreau,
*Walden: Or, Life in the Woods*

*When anxious, uneasy and bad thoughts come, I
go to the sea, and the sea drowns them out with its
great wide sounds, cleanses me with its noise, and
imposes a rhythm upon everything in me that is
bewildered and confused.*

—Rainer Maria Rilke

*The sea does not reward those who are too anxious,
too greedy, or too impatient. One should lie empty,
open, choiceless as a beach—waiting for a gift from
the sea.*

—Anne Morrow Lindbergh,
*Gift from the Sea*

# Happy Day Calendar

Pick something you really want to celebrate. Select a date, and declare it a holiday—*your* holiday. Invite friends over. Create slogans. Make up a new "traditional dish" for the holiday. Cut up an old sheet and paint a flag on it for your holiday. Do you have an unofficial song, too? If so, sing it!

Standard calendars in the United States come already marked with Memorial Day, Labor Day, and Independence Day. Why not make your own Happy Days calendar that includes your self-declared holiday? Make sure you add your birthday and your friends' birthdays, too.

What's something you like? Air conditioning? Flying? When was it invented? Add that date to your Happy Days calendar.

Here are some additional celebration days you may want to put on your Happy Days calendar for some future glee:

| | |
|---|---|
| January 12: | National Hug Day |
| March 20: | International Happiness Day |
| First Sunday in May: | World Laughter Day |
| July 30: | International Friendship Day |
| September 21: | International Peace Day |
| August 19: | World Humanitarian Day |
| November 13: | World Kindness Day |

# International Happiness Day

OF COURSE, MAKING EVERY DAY A CELEBRATION IS A WAY to be happy daily, but in case you want to go celebrate globally, put a star near March 20 on your calendar. That's the official International Happiness Day!

Back in 2011, the sixty-sixth session of the United Nations General Assembly resolved that "...the pursuit of happiness is a fundamental human goal," and that happiness should be recognized in public policy aims around the world.

So the UN declared that March 20 could be dedicated "to observe the International Day of Happiness in an appropriate manner, including through education and public awareness–raising activities." Websites, happiness clubs, apps, and activities sprung up. Some nations are examining the role of happiness in their public policies.

In 2014, Happiness Day inspired the world's first twenty-four-hour music video. The song was Pharrell's "Happy," of course, and video material was supplied from folks around the world.

Do you have a project to contribute to Happiness Day? Can you say Happy Happy Day?

# Europe Report

Released on International Happiness Day (March 20) in 2015, the first-ever Eurostat Survey of the Happiness of European Nations announced its national happiness rankings, based on three areas:

**Affects** – The presence of positive feelings and lack of negative feelings

**Eudaimonics** – The sense that one's life has meaning and purpose

**Life Satisfaction**

Like similar surveys, happiness here is largely gauged by "subjective well-being" (SWB—emotional and cognitive), with participants rating their own answers on a one-to-ten scale.

Denmark, Finland, Sweden, and Switzerland all tied for the top four spots. Iceland and Norway tied for the fifth and sixth slots. Bulgaria came in last with an overall 4.8 average.

Here are some other findings from the survey:

- The single greatest indicator of happiness and unhappiness in the survey was health, not income.
- Younger people were happier than older.
- Men and women were about equally satisfied with life overall.
- The inactive and unemployed were generally the least satisfied, and people in education and training rated themselves as the happiest of the employed.

# Arbejdsglaede

*ARBEJDSGLAEDE* IS A DANISH WORD THAT MEANS "HAPPINESS at work," or work-gladness and joy—something beyond job satisfaction. Alexander Kjerulf, the Chief Happiness Officer of Wohoo, says that only the Scandinavian languages have this word, and he has made it his mission to make the word and concept global.

He says *arbejdsglaede* (pronounced ah-BITES-gleh-the) is about liking the people you work with, making a difference, doing well, and looking forward to Monday morning. It's good for you and the workplace, he posits. The research he has studied shows that happier people, on average, are more creative, resilient, and successful, and that happier companies tend to make more money and have stocks that do well.

To achieve *arbejdsglaede*, it takes a different Three Rs:
Relationships + Results + Responsibility = Work Happiness

The responsibility part is you—not a boss or corporate rules. *You*, he urges, are responsible for your work happiness.

Others say the Dutch word *arbeidsvreugde* is close. Germans have *arbeitszufriedenheit*, which is more about satisfaction.

Do you know of other languages that have "work happiness" as a word? How's your *arbejdsglaede*?

ALEX KJERULF URGES THAT IT'S WORTH THE EFFORTS to make your workday happy, since you may spend more time at work than with family, friends, and hobbies combined.

According to Kjerulf, some quick tips that work at work around the world include:

- Start your day with a fabulous "Good Morning" to co-workers; make them glad they are at work, too.

- Celebrate the victories while they come, instead of focusing on what's wrong.

- Before you leave work for the day, write down three things about the day that made you happy.

For more from this *arbejdsglaede* evangelist, check out his blog—*Chief Happiness Officer*, at positivesharing.com.

# Meditate

MEDITATION CAN HELP YOU MASTER THE MYRIAD OF worries and fears that clutter and agitate our brain, feed troubling physical results, and impair happiness. Meditation can also lead to great peace, insight, and, for some, enlightenment.

Like many practices and skills, meditation takes time to master. There are also many different types of meditation, from ancient Hindu practices to modern ones aimed at specific imbalances. You need to find which is best for you. Don't give up if the first type you try isn't a fit.

The simplest form of meditation is to modify something you do all the time: breathe.

If you are ready, take a deep breath, exhale, and try the tips on the following pages.

Some of the benefits attributed to meditation include:

- Lower blood pressure

- Lower cholesterol

- Lower anxiety

- Reduced asthma symptoms

- Increased resiliency against stress

- Increased ability to fall asleep and to sleep better

- Increased brain synchronicity

- Increased mental focus and clarity

- Increased serotonin for better moods

- Improved intuition abilities

- Improved immune system

# Breathing

About ten million times a year, we breathe.

Those breaths keep us alive. They can also help us be happier, according to research and traditions, if we make them the focus of meditation.

Try sitting straight. Close your eyes, and see if you can just think about your breath for a few minutes. Do not latch on to any other thoughts that try to dominate (and they will!). Just think about your breath.

Try breathing only through your nose. Be aware of what happens if you slow down a bit and take longer on both the inhalations and exhalations.

Don't be upset with yourself if niggling thoughts try to steal your focus, or if you suddenly think you need to write something down to remember it.

Can you go thirty seconds without thoughts interfering with your focus on your breath? Can you go longer each time you try?

One way to start is to count your breaths. Think "one" as you breathe in and as you breathe out. Then think "two" both in and out. What number can you count to without another thought pirouetting in or another worry dive-bombing your focus?

Smile, and start again.

If counting doesn't work for you, try repeating a phrase (or mantra) you like.

# The 2,600-Year-Old Breathing Tip

*When I discovered the Discourse on the Full Awareness of Breathing, I felt I was the happiest person on Earth. These exercises have been transmitted by a community that has been practicing for 2,600 years.*

—Thich Nhat Hanh

THE DISCOURSE, FOUND IN THE ANAPANASATI SUTTA, AN ancient Indian text, is a specific path to enlightenment using breath. It includes words credited to the Buddha himself.

An English translation of one section may be something you want to repeat mentally while breathing slowly:

- Breathing in, I feel joyful. Breathing out, I feel joyful.

- Breathing in, I feel happy. Breathing out, I feel happy.

Try letting these words, which are part of a larger practice that has been handed down through millennia, fill your brain and being as your breath rises and falls in your body.

It's a free tonic and a powerful tool for happiness that has passed the test of time with many generations.

# Count

*Count your age by friends, not years.*
*Count your life by smiles, not tears.*

THESE POPULAR LINES ARE OFTEN CREDITED TO JOHN
Lennon of the Beatles, but they were written before he was
born. A *New Yorker* article by E.B. White in 1935 says the
author was the wife of another famous singer and cultural
icon—Bing Crosby.

The lines were part of a longer poem in a very
successful greeting card. Dixie Lee Crosby was reputedly
paid a flat fee of $5, not royalties. Hopefully, she counted
her wealth in deeds, not dollars.

The couplet is still a good start to count what counts
for your blessings and happiness.

# Love

*Love knows no limits, but ardently transcends all bounds. Love feels no burden, takes no account of toil, attempts things beyond its strength; love sees nothing as impossible, for it feels able to achieve all things. Love therefore does great things; it is strange and effective; while he who lacks love faints and fails."*

       –Thomas à Kempis, *The Imitation of Christ*

*There is only one happiness in this life, to love and be loved.*

       –George Sand

FROM THOUSANDS OF YEARS BEFORE THE MEDIEVAL writings of spiritual author à Kempis, to the Beatles' "All You Need is Love," and probably for thousands of years yet to come, love has been both a source and a fulfillment of happiness.

Love can be the instrument, musician, and composer of happiness.

Divine love, self love, compassionate love for all beings, romantic love—all of these can be paths to happiness and the results of happiness.

How do love and happiness intertwine in your life?

Try closing your eyes, thinking of someone you love, and imagining a happy time together.

# I Love You

THOSE THREE POWERFUL WORDS CAN MAKE ANYBODY'S day—parents, kids, or friends.

When is the last time you said "I love you" in a new way?

Have you tried a note in the refrigerator? Or lunch bag? Or purse? Or golf club bag?

What about a little vase with a fresh flower in one of the cupholders of his or her car?

Other ideas:

Mail a mushy card to somebody you love on an ordinary day, so a sweet surprise waits in the mail.

Without prompting, do a chore your loved one abhors.

If you get home first, have your loved one's favorite music playing as a personal welcome home.

Give a handmade gift certificate for something your loved one would really like. It could be anything from a foot rub to baseball tickets, just make sure it's something that is wanted, not just something you want to give.

# Wonder Junkie

*She was a wonder junkie. In her mind, she was a*
*hill tribesman standing slack-jawed before the real*
*Ishtar Gate of ancient Babylon; Dorothy catching*
*her first glimpse of the vaulted spires of the*
*Emerald City of Oz…she was Pocahontas sailing*
*up the Thames estuary with London spread out*
*before her from horizon to horizon.*

—Carl Sagan, *Contact*

CARL SAGAN, THE MAN WHO PRECEDED DR. NEIL DEGRASSE Tyson in bringing cosmic wonder to popular audiences, coined the phrase "Wonder Junkie."

Collecting wonders doesn't need to take up space like a doll or car collection, but it can provide intangible touchstones to delight and contentment. It can live in one's imagination from great stories, or be a collection of actual memories from both exotic exploration and the extraordinary of ordinary daily life.

To collect Wonders, you may decide to plot a trip halfway around the globe to experience something rare, like paddling in a mangrove surrounded by synchronous fireflies blinking on and off in unison. Or, you might simply take a walk at your local park and notice real "ducks in a row," lined up in front of a shimmering lake.

World Wide Wonder can be your www. How wonder-full!

# Useful

*No one is useless in this world who lightens the burdens of another.*

—Charles Dickens

MOST PEOPLE WANT TO BE "WELL USED" IN LIFE, TO HAVE their value add to the world around them. Purpose and meaning are key elements in a layer of happiness that goes deeper and extends longer than a cold drink on a hot afternoon. But you can be useful by giving someone a cold beverage when needed. Let moments add to meaning. Not everyone can find a cure for a disease every day, but each of us can be useful.

If you thoughtfully perform five acts of kindness in a day, one study shows, your whole week will be happier. You can lighten the burdens of others—and lighten your mood. Try it where you work.

*Always desire to learn something useful.*

—Sophocles

MAKE SURE YOU ARE USEFUL, BUT NOT USED UP. ANOTHER study shows that employees who work overtime regularly and more often than their colleagues are often less happy and are promoted less. Sometimes quality is better than quantity.

To give your best in creativity and productivity at work, you need to make sure you also have time to rest, to play, and to be with loved ones—then you can give to them in different ways, and receive richly.

Of course, with the proper balance, there's no reason you still can't perform those five acts of kindness in a day at work.

One of the most useful things you can do for your happiness is figure out how you can be best useful.

# Happy Co.

THE HAPPIEST COMPANIES IN AMERICA FOR 2015, according to CareerBliss.com, are Johnson & Johnson, Broadcom, Texas Instruments, McAfee, Google, Intuit, Adobe, Amgen, and SAP AG (in that order).

CareerBliss bases its results on company reviews from thousands of people who visit its website, so the results are biased in favor of those who know the site and will take time to do the surveys. Nevertheless, the process encourages you to think about the qualities of a happy workplace.

The scores are then averaged to give a company its final grade.

In the CareerBliss survey, people were asked to rate the following factors:

- work-life balance

- relationship with boss and coworkers

- work environment

- job resources

- compensation

- growth opportunities

- company culture

- company reputation

- daily tasks

- job control over daily work

Do you think any key factors are left out of the equation? How would you revise it?

How would you rate your workplace?

# Happy Words

*laughter, happiness, love, happy, laughed, laugh, laughing, excellent, laughs, joy, successful, win, rainbow, smile, won, pleasure, smiled, rainbows, winning, celebration*
—The top twenty happy words in English, according to a university study

A RESEARCH TEAM FROM THE MATH, STATISTICS, AND computer departments at the University of Vermont wanted to find out what the happiest words are in the English language, and whether we use happy or sad words more often.

First, they determined what the ten thousand most frequently used English words are these days, relying on the *New York Times*, Google Books Library Project, Twitter, and music lyrics as sources. Then they had people rate the words on a scale of one to ten, according to how positive they perceived the words to be.

The findings were that there is a "positivity bias." People use far more "happy" or positive words than they do negative words.

# Positivity Bias

IN RESEARCH PUBLISHED IN 2015, A STUDY OF TEN DIVERSE languages showed that each had more positive words than negative ones, and the positive words within the languages were used more frequently than the negative ones. "Average word happiness" was also positive in every language.

The results, published in the *Proceedings of the National Academy of Sciences*, showed a "universal positivity bias."

Native speakers of Arabic, Brazilian Portuguese, Chinese, English, French, German, Indonesian, Korean, Spanish, and Russian were all asked to report whether they felt positively or negatively about words presented. Five million individual scores were evaluated. The vocabulary words were pulled from popular Internet sites, songs, and books. Spanish and Brazilian Portuguese were the happiest languages in the study.

The research confirmed "The Pollyanna Hypotheses" first formulated in 1969, which proposed that people across cultures tend to use positive words more often than negative words. Relatively small studies led to the hypothesis then, but now "big data" can be used to confirm that it's true.

# States of Well-Being

IN THE ANNUAL GALLUP-HEALTHWAYS WELL-BEING INDEX survey, residents from all fifty United States are asked to report about their daily lives. The survey refers to itself as "the most proven, mature, and comprehensive measure of well-being in populations."

The survey uses a "holistic" approach to measure well-being, gathering data in five areas:

- **Purpose:** Whether people like what they do each day and are motivated to achieve their goals

- **Social:** Whether people's lives include supportive relationships and love

- **Financial:** How well people reduce stress and increase security by managing their economic lives

- **Community:** Whether people like, feel safe, and are proud of where they live

- **Physical:** Whether people are healthy and energetic enough to complete daily tasks

The surveyors have found that communities with high measures of well-being use health care less often and miss less work, among other things.

On a scale of one to one hundred, how would you rank

your life in each of the areas above? How different are "well-being" and "happiness" to you?

ACCORDING TO THE 2014 GALLUP-HEALTHWAYS WELL-Being Index, for the first time, Alaska has the best "State of Well-Being." West Virginia came in last of the fifty states, and Kentucky was number forty-nine.

Geographically, it is interesting to note that, except for the two states physically disconnected from the rest of the country (Alaska and Hawaii), the other eight states ranked among the top ten (Montana, South Dakota, Wyoming, Nebraska, Colorado, Utah, New Mexico, and Texas) all cover a solid stretch of land through the middle of the country, from Canada to Mexico.

Only two states (Hawaii and Colorado) have been in the top ten every year since the Gallup-Healthways survey began in 2008. West Virginia and Kentucky have consistently been in the bottom ten.

Are West Virginians and Kentuckians simply more modest in how they perceive themselves, so they rate themselves lower? Do they measure their well-being and happiness using different standards? Or should we send the residents of those states a copy of this book?

# Inside Job

**Throughout the centuries, many people have suggested that happiness is an "inside job."**

*The happiness of your life depends on the quality of your thoughts.*

> —Marcus Aurelius, *Meditations*

*Happiness...depends on what lies between the sole of your foot and the crown of your head; and whether it costs a million or a hundred louis, the actual amount of pleasure that you receive rests entirely with you, and is just exactly the same in any case.*

> —Honoré de Balzac, *Father Goriot* (1835)

*Our principles are the springs of our actions. Our actions, the springs of our happiness and misery. Too much care, therefore, cannot be employed in forming our principles.*

> —*The National Magazine,*
> "Thoughts to Think About," January 1855

*Happiness is the greatest paradox in Nature. It can grow in any soil, live under any conditions. It defies environment. It comes from within.*

> —William George Jordan,
> "The Royal Road to Happiness" (1928)

*A man is happy so long as he chooses to be happy and nothing can stop him.*

—Aleksandr Solzhenitsyn

*Happiness is living by inner purpose, not by outside pressures.*

—David Augsburger, professor,
Fuller Theological Seminary

*Happiness is within us, and it is ours, but we are always superimposing our own inner joy onto something outside and thinking it comes from there.*

—Swami Muktananda

*A happy person is not a person in a certain set of circumstances, but rather a person with a certain set of attitudes.*

—Hugh Downs

*When you discover that all happiness is inside you, the wanting and needing are over.*

Byron Katie, "The Work"

# Star Light

SEEK OUT THE STARS. NOURISH YOUR SPIRIT WITH THE SAME stellar night-lights seen by the earliest humans, the first Olympic athletes, the best minds of the Renaissance, and your great-great-grandparents. Depending on where you live, you may see different specific stars, but still feel the same awe and connectedness.

The lights of most cities and suburbs block our ability to see many stars. But the stars are still there—just as answers are often "there" for us to find, but lost in the clutteredness and artificial lights of our modern lives. Head to the dark for the wonder of starlight—the illumination of uncountable suns twinkling in the vast blackness.

If you have a backyard, turn off your houselights at night, tilt back a chair outside, and cup your hands to the sides of your eyes to block out sidelights. Then, look up and wait.

Give your eyes time to adjust, and more and more stars may be revealed. And perhaps with the lights in the dark, you will feel the peacefulness and happiness known to poets, sailors, and shepherds through the ages.

# Star Bright

WE ARE ALL MADE OF STARDUST. EVERYTHING ON EARTH IS composed of the same elements found in stars, so communing with them can be, well, elemental. But it's not always easy.

If artificial light "pollution" and sky glow make it hard for you to see the splendor overhead where you live, you can find a dark-sky preserve. First created in Canada, dark-sky preserves are often around big parks or observatories and can be great for stargazing.

If you are in a remote area or out at sea for vacation, don't forget to look up at night to feel more up.

You might not only see the glory of the heavens, but also catch the ride of a falling star. Of course, the stars aren't really falling. Falling stars are actually meteors entering the earth's atmosphere, heating up, glowing brightly, then disintegrating. They are nature's fireworks.

Some people believe that if you make a wish on the first star of the night, or when a falling star is arcing its way, the wish will come true. In the quiet dark with pinpricks of twinkling lights, our elemental wishes can become clearer. What are yours? How do you make them come true?

# Deep Silence

*Happiness is silence. Sit quietly and listen. Your senses become more acute, and eventually nature reveals itself. Like any skill, this requires constant practice. Be happy, be quiet.*

—Don Walsh

OCEANOGRAPHER AND EXPLORER CAPTAIN DON WALSH dove more than thirty-five thousand feet into the Pacific Ocean in the Navy's bathyscaphe *Trieste* in 1960. The place was the Challenger Deep, the deepest part in the World Ocean. In 2012, Dr. Walsh joined the team that helped James Cameron revisit those depths in the Mariana Trench for one of his deep-sea documentaries. For more than five decades, Walsh has been involved with the exploration of the deep oceans and polar regions of our planet. Walsh has received the highest honors from the Explorers Club and the National Geographic Society. He continues to lead expeditions—when he isn't sitting quietly, and happily.

# High Choice

*HAPPINESS IS A CONSCIOUS DECISION, GENERALLY speaking. By and large, life deals us a healthy mix of easy and hard, wins and losses, and it's in how we decide to process this turbulence that determines our "happiness quotient." When I'm talking to young people about the opportunities and challenges of our current day, I actually describe my proverbial cup, not as half-full and certainly not half-empty; more like three-quarters-to-overflowing-full!*

*So what's my personal secret formula that drives such a conscious act, to derive happiness from the various curveballs of life?*

*Optimism, of course, and a general distrust of naysayers. [Those who said I could never beat the odds and become an astronaut or never succeed at climbing Mount Everest were immediately removed from my Christmas card list!] Add to this a relentless curiosity about the world, with a desire for challenge and adventure, as well as engagement with other people and other ideas. And, most importantly, a deep reciprocal loving relationship with my wife, wonderful family, and closest friends fuels me. Love conquers all…*

—Dr. Scott Parazynski,
whose many accomplishments include five space
flights, seven space walks, inventing, a Stanford
medical degree, and being the only astronaut to
summit Mount Everest, Earth's highest point.

# Happiness Quizzes

THE UNIVERSITY OF PENNSYLVANIA RUNS THE AUTHENTIC Happiness website, which offers multiple questionnaires that anyone can take for free. Results are immediate and include bar graphs and percentages that tell you how your answers compare to others of your gender, level of education, age range, occupation, and even zip code.

With the "Approaches to Happiness" survey, you can see how you compare to others in three areas of happiness:

- Meaningful Life (serving more than yourself)

- Good Life (applying your strengths well)

- Pleasant Life (packing in the pleasures and enjoying them)

The research indicates that high scores in the Pleasant Life category do not add up to what they call the "Satisfaction of Life" scale, but a Good Life and Meaningful Life do.

To help you learn more about your happiness through the lens of positive psychology, there are also questionnaires on strength, grit, optimism, and gratitude.

The site measures only your current state of mind, and it encourages users to come back and test again to see how their statuses change.

Remember though, do not make yourself unhappy by comparing yourself to others, or by setting up unrealistic expectations for yourself. All tools can be used for positive or negative aims. Learning about your strengths can help your journey.

# Lines

YOU ARE STANDING WITH A BUNCH OF OTHER PEOPLE WHO probably also don't want to be waiting in line. It's easy to gripe unfairly about the slow postal worker or the fumbling cashier, or the idiot (fill in the blank). Why not share some glow or giggles, instead of grump and glower?

Maybe ask a question relevant to the situation, like "How do you cook asparagus?" (a question better-suited for the market checkout line than for a movie ticket line).

Or, if you are genuine, give a compliment: "I love your blue sweater. Where did you get it?"

Look around and see if you can help anybody, or think of a way to help the line move faster.

You may get other folks' minds off the wait, as well as your own. And, in making strangers feel good, you could make yourself feel good as well.

# More Happy Lines

MAYBE YOU ARE STUCK ON A LINE AND YOU DON'T FEEL like conversing. Don't worry. There are also nonverbal ways you can make sure "wait" doesn't mean "waste." Here are some clues for better cues:

- Start a chain reaction of smiles—let your eyes and lips send good cheer to the person next to you. Perhaps that person will spread the smile to another, and before long the entire line will be smiling.

- Hum a catchy happy tune, or do some slow stretches and see if others join in.

- Think kind thoughts for the person who is working at the destination of the line—some compassion for the person who will be helping all of you (hopefully) soon.

- Breathe in slowly and deeply—the air of someone who realizes the line is an opportunity to slow down and replace rush with rejuvenation.

# Long Life

Groucho Marx was the longtime host of the mid-twentieth-century TV quiz show *You Bet Your Life*. Of the hundreds of contestants he interviewed, Groucho said one of his favorites was a guest in March of 1951—Hannus Von Yannah, a 102-year-old Norwegian.

When Groucho asked Hannus for his secret, he replied:

*I think the secret to longevity is to be happy. Every day a man wakes up, he has the choice whether he will be happy or unhappy. I have chosen to be happy.*

Groucho responded, "That's a wonderful philosophy."

# Imagination

PUT ON SOME MUSIC AND JUST DANCE. SING LOUDLY. WAVE your arms and pretend to conduct an orchestra or to extol your opinions in an address to Congress.

Sit in a chair and imagine you are driving in the Indy 500, or straddle a bench and gallop to victory in the Kentucky Derby.

Even if all that does is get you to laugh, you have catapulted yourself out of any doldrums.

Or maybe you would rather lie on the grass in a park or snuggle into warm sands and pretend you are...floating on a cloud or on the back of a whale? Being frozen to wake up in the year 2200? A sleeping prince or princess waiting for a kiss to wake up in a fairytale?

The imagination, delight, and play we enjoyed as children doesn't have to perish. There are times your imagination may be a happier, closer nation than any other country you can visit.

# Swing

Swing in a hammock.

    Sway gently, mid-air, suspended between trees or posts.

    Let something else hold you up.

    Rock like a sleeping baby in a cradle

           or a dreamer on a ship at sea under the stars.

    Flow like the tides in and out, back and forth on the shore.

    Free and easy.

    Let life be.

    Take off your shoes and jump on a swing in a park.

    Arc up and up with your toes stretched out.

    Tickle the trees with your toes—or the clouds, or the moon.

    Tickle your fancy.

    Laugh with the best echoes of childhood, with the
freedom of flying through space.

# Six Factors to Improve Health and Happiness

RESEARCHERS AT ENGLAND'S UNIVERSITY OF ESSEX suggest that people would generally be happier if society moved toward environmentally sustainable consumption, even though it might not be good for the economy.

According to their study, released in 2015, the negative health effects of material consumption cost the United Kingdom economy more than $273 billion each year. Such costs include spending on mental ill-health, dementia, obesity, physical inactivity, diabetes, loneliness, and cardiovascular disease.

They recommend that a focus on six specific factors would improve a society's health and happiness:

healthy food
physical activity
mental wellness
strong community and family ties
time spent in nature
attachment to meaningful possessions

# Happy Wall

READY TO BE A GRAFFITI ARTIST OF SORTS TO COMBINE
gratitude, glee, and creativity?

There's the Wailing Wall in Jerusalem; a prayer
wall outside the home honoring Jesus's mother Mary in
Ephesus, Turkey; a wall of immigrants' names at Ellis Island;
and many other important memorial walls.

Why not a Happy Wall that *you* create?

On International Happiness Day in March 2015,
orange-colored Happiness Walls popped up in different
schools and cities in North America for the day. People
were encouraged to post a card with a Happiness Act—one
of the initiatives of *Live Happy* magazine—and the media
spread the words.

You could create a personal Happy Wall at home to
support your well-being year-round. You and your friends
might also want to start a community wall that stands up, so
to speak, for happiness in daily life. Pick the local colors or
your favorite ones.

HERE ARE SOME IDEAS YOU CAN ADOPT OR ADAPT OR FORGET for your Happy Wall. You could use a corkboard with pins or a whiteboard with pens and tape to create special areas, such as:

- **Gratitude:** Photos and words expressing what you are grateful for, past and present

- **Inspiration:** Quotes and articles and things that teach and inspire happiness

- **Love:** Cards from friends, drawings from children, and more photos

- **Engagement:** Awards, certificates of participation, upcoming things you want to do, photos of actions you and others have taken to make others happy

- **Reminders:** Things that help you with habits you want for health and happiness

- **Humor:** Draw goofy faces, put up comics and cartoons, post photos of people you love making funny faces

What else? You decide! Each member of your family could have their own section of the wall, so you can cheer each other on. In your living area, you will have created a wall among you that unites, not divides.

# Onboard

You could also think big, and get your community or social group to post a happy board full of good news and happy moments and gratitude cards. Have school kids and prominent community members write what makes them happy and also what they do to make others happy. What are people's definitions of happiness? What is a "happiest memory" in the town?

Imagine walking into your city hall and reading contributions about places to get a great view in your town, about the kindness of a neighbor, or about upcoming opportunities to volunteer.

Maybe suggest posting a whiteboard with colored pens at your local coffee shop, recreation center, yoga studio, or doctor's waiting area, so others can participate in happiness in the moment with endearing quotes and original thoughts.

Help people be "onboard" with sharing happiness.

# Happy Hour

FOR MOST PEOPLE, HAPPY HOUR CONJURES CLINKING glasses at bargain prices at a bar in the late afternoon.

The social habit of a happy hour (or two), of drinking before dinner, began when the goals of Prohibition backfired. In 1920, the Eighteenth Amendment to the Constitution and the Volstead Act prohibited producing and selling alcohol throughout the United States. Since people couldn't enjoy alcohol when they dined in restaurants, they met earlier in private at illegal "speakeasies" for what were called "cocktail hours" or "happy hours."

In 1933, that Eighteenth Amendment made history by being the only amendment to be repealed completely. And people are still cheering at happy hours everywhere.

But according to the findings of Harvard's Grant Study, the truly happy drinkers are those who only drink moderately and have mastered the art of loving and being loved. Abuse of alcohol was the most common cause of divorce and marital unhappiness among the people studied during a seventy-five-year period. The report also revealed that depression didn't cause alcoholism, but that alcoholism is a cause of depression.

Bottom line, instead of bottoms up: More laughing and talking, and less gulping, can let your happy hour be happy for more than an hour.

# Sunset

THERE ARE PLACES IN THE WORLD WHERE PEOPLE STOP FOR the sunset—to pay homage to the beauty and to say thanks for the gift of another day lived.

On the coast of Punta del Este in Uruguay, at the whimsical, whitewashed home and gallery of artist Carlos Páez Vilaró, everyone is handed champagne or juice as sunset approaches. Vilaro's voice, recorded before he died, shares a poetic ode to the sun as that glorious star glides into the sea and paints the sky.

Glasses clink and people clap at Casapueblo. Strangers bond over the beauty of the sun swallowed by the sea— another day given and spent. It's a collective, connective passage.

Pausing for the ancient punctuation of nature, for the timeless rhythms amidst our boisterous cacophony of humanity, is an organic way to let the happy hour last much longer than sixty minutes.

# Strangers

*There are no strangers here; Only friends you haven't yet met.*

—William Butler Yeats

DO YOU THINK YOU WOULD BE HAPPIER ENJOYING SOLITUDE on your commuter train ride or starting a conversation with a stranger?

Strangely, researchers have learned through multiple studies about happiness that people often are not good at predicting what makes them happy.

People in one study predicted they would be happier being alone than they would be conversing with someone they had never met. Yet, when behavioral scientists asked them to strike up a conversation, the participants who did later reported feeling happier than when they were alone.

Put this one to the test yourself. Conduct your own experiment. Start a conversation with a stranger. Did you learn that social interactions create good feelings? Were Yeats and the researchers right?

# New Friends

*You can make more friends in two months by becoming interested in other people than you can in two years by trying to get other people interested in you.*

—Dale Carnegie,
*How to Win Friends and Influence People*

CARNEGIE WROTE HIS BEST SELLER YEARS BEFORE POSITIVE psychology showed that one's social network is a good indicator of and source for health and happiness. Making friends isn't always easy at any age, though, and as Carnegie said, trying to get people to like you is not the most effective path for friendship and connection. Instead, try finding out what *you* might like about the *other* person and letting that other person feel liked.

One of the best ways to engage other people is to ask good questions and then be a good listener. Try not to interrupt with your story (even if you think it is better). Most people love to talk about themselves. Some rarely get a chance to be really *listened* to, and they will think you are smart and wonderful if your ears work more than your lips.

# Questions

YEARS AGO, A SMART, SINGLE WOMAN (LET'S CALL HER Marsha) had a test at parties and social gatherings when it came to getting to know strangers. If, after five or ten minutes of conversation, the other person hadn't asked her a single question, but had only talked about himself, Marsha politely excused herself and went to meet someone else.

She was good at asking questions, a skilled listener, and genuinely curious about other people. But she had learned the hard way that people who didn't ask questions of others tended to be self-absorbed. She wanted curiosity to be a two-way street. She wanted to be with people who could care about her the way she might care about them.

In addition to using her litmus test on others, you might want to monitor yourself in conversations, whether it's a singles dating mash-up or a family reunion. Can you make the chatter cheerier for others by asking questions about them? And then follow up by being good at listening to the answers?

This woman, by the way, ended up marrying a big-time magazine editor who asks questions for a living. And they seem to live happily. Just ask them!

# Thanks-Giving in July

THE UNITED STATES NOT ONLY HAS THE "PURSUIT OF happiness" in its constitution, it has a national holiday for "thanks-giving," which modern researchers say is one of the surest paths to happiness.

Sometimes, though, the attitude of gratitude gets lost between the gravy and the stresses of travel logistics, holiday pressures, impossible expectations, and, of course, football on TV. You may change that for the November holiday in the future, and you may be great about daily gratitude. Or you may live somewhere that *doesn't* have a day dedicated to Thanksgiving.

Why not develop another opportunity to have a feast with thanks in the relaxed glows of summer? Bring together some of your favorite foods and people, and gather with conscious gratitude. You can create your own tradition without commercialism. Go around the table and let each person fill in the blank with grace: "I am thankful for_____ ."

Yes, it's corny and sweet. Maybe that, and the sheer pleasure of looking around at people you love, will make good companions to your juicy corn on the cob and sweet ice cream.

# Ceremony

*The varieties of happiness in Judaism are embedded in rituals and cultural codes that are part of the very fabric of being a Jew.*

*I think most of all about a central passage in the Jewish ceremony, where the seven blessings over the wedding couple include the idea that God has created* sasson *and* simcha—glee, *lyrical happiness, abundant pleasure, exultation, and so on.*

*Then there is the almost routine greeting that Jews use at festival time:* Chag Sameach—"a happy festival." *"The common response is* Hagim u'zmanim lesasson— *"And may all your festivals and seasons be joyous"— using the two words from the wedding ceremony.*

*A happiness hyperbole is also found in the word* tsohala—"exuberant happiness"—*which, like so many Hebrew nouns, can become a verb by the simple readjustment of vowels.*

*Hebrew may not have the market cornered on having many words for "happiness", but perhaps the special cultural signals implied in each different form of the words for "happiness", and the occasions they remind us of, make Judaism and Hebrew a little special, even if not entirely unique.*

—William Cutter, Rabbi, Ph.D.,
Hebrew Union College-Jewish Institute of
Religion, Los Angeles, California

# Prayer

*You pray in your distress and in your need; would
that you might pray also in the fullness of your joy
and in your days of abundance. For what is prayer
but the expansion of your self into the living ether?*
—Kahlil Gibran, *The Prophet*

DICTIONARIES SAY "TO PRAY" IS:

• to offer thanks and praise to God or a deity or
object of worship

• to ask for, petition, or entreat

• to make a solemn request (often for others)

• to devoutly wish

• to enter into a spiritual communion with God or a
subject of worship

Researchers now say that prayer is also the most
popular form of alternative medicine in the country. People
who pray and/or meditate tend to be healthier, to live
longer, and to report being happier. It's not clear which way
the arrows go for cause and effect, but prayer is correlated
with health and happiness.

*If the only prayer you said in your whole life was "thank you," that would suffice.*

—Meister Eckhart

BESIDES THE DIVINE POSSIBILITIES, RESEARCH HAS SHOWN that prayer can help the person praying achieve a "relaxation response." Physiologically, brain waves slow and blood pressure goes down, while tranquility and the sense of control go up.

According to the Pew Research Center, 5 percent of those surveyed say they pray daily.

Another Pew study concluded that 76 percent of Americans surveyed agree with the statement, "Prayer is an important part of my daily life." This has held relatively steady over twenty-five years of surveys.

Even among those who say they are "not affiliated with a religion," 21 percent say they pray daily, and 8 percent of people who have a major illness pray.

According to a University of Virginia study, couples who pray together have happier relationships.

# Happiness Gods

THROUGHOUT HISTORY, HUMANS HAVE TURNED TO THE Divine for happiness. Many cultures with multiple deities have a god or goddess of happiness.

In Greek mythology, Euphrosyne was one of three triplet daughters of Zeus known as the Three Graces. The Grace of Delight, or the Goddess of Mirth, she was usually pictured dancing with her sisters and attending to Aphrodite (Goddess of Beauty) and Eros (God of Love). Her counterpart in Roman mythology, Felicitas, was often depicted on the coins of Rome, because emperors wanted to be thought of as providing happiness to their people.

In sixth-century China, Yang Cheng was a local official in Hunan province at a time when the emperor, solely for his amusement, took little people of that region to serve in the palace. When the emperor sent for more children, Yang Cheng refused, saying the little people were not slaves. The emperor, impressed with Yang Cheng's arguments and his bravery, agreed to stop and to return all the little people. From that day forward, Yang Cheng's people deified him. He became Fu Xing, the God of Happiness, and one of the three star gods of good fortune.

# Laughter

IN SIXTEENTH-CENTURY JAPAN, HOTEI, A LARGE MAN WITH a big belly, traveled the countryside—laughing. Hotei was known for his irrepressible, contagious laughter. Although he did not preach, he was revered as a master who taught people to achieve enlightenment through laughter. Once, when Hotei was sitting quietly under a tree with his eyes closed, the story goes, that a villager asked why Hotei was not laughing. Hotei replied:

> I have to prepare myself for laughter. I have to rest. I have to go within. I have to forget the whole world so that I can recharge, and then I can be filled with laughter again.

"The Laughing Buddha" is now considered one of Japan's Seven Lucky Gods.

# Happiness Deities

GODDESSES OF HAPPINESS ABOUND IN DIFFERENT CULTURES, representing various aspects of happiness to honor or petition:

- Ekajata is a Buddhist and Hindu goddess of joy and happiness and removing obstacles.

- An Indian goddess of playfulness and pleasure, Lalita, sees the universe as her playground.

- Samkhat was a Babylonian goddess of happiness and joy.

Other gods of happiness include:

- The Slavic god Belun, the bringer of good luck and god of heavenly light, peace, and happiness

- Re'are'a, a Tahitian god of happiness and joy

- Tsho-gyalma, a Tibetan god of happiness

- Wopeh, the Lakota god of happiness and pleasure

- Ururupuin, the Micronesian god of flirting, happiness, and playfulness

# Giving

*It's not how much we give but how much love we put into giving.*

—Mother Teresa

IN OLDER MARRIED COUPLES, THE HUSBANDS OR WIVES WHO give usually live longer—whether it's emotional nurturing to their spouses or active support to friends, neighbors, and other family. This was one of the gems from a five-year study of older couples that suggests generosity of time and heart has its own rewards. The study, "Providing Social Support May Be More Beneficial Than Receiving It," reported in *Psychological Science*, suggests something known by many religions: Give and you receive.

In any relationship, at any age, do you try to give more than you take?

# Happy New Year

THE NEW YEAR IS A CHANCE TO START AGAIN. HOW CAN you make it a "happy" year? How can you resolve any lingering problems? Taking time to make New Year's resolutions may go back several thousand years to the Babylonians (perhaps as early as 2,600 B.C.). Having goals to aim for, but not setting expectations for yourself too high, is a delicate balance.

The founder of the *Old Farmer's Almanac* (started in 1792, and still going) recommended a different kind of balance:

> *Begin the new year square with every man.*
> —Robert B. Thomas

Today that could mean being squared away financially and emotionally with everyone, including yourself!

(As for the resolutions, don't stress too much about them. The Babylonians probably haven't stuck to theirs, either.)

IN MANY CULTURES, CERTAIN FOOD TRADITIONS ARE USED to help make the new year a happy one.

In Dutch homes, a fried circular sweet called *olle bollen* is served. Any round food represents "coming full circle," which is believed to lead to good fortune.

In India or Pakistan, eating rice for the new year portends prosperity.

For some in the southern United States, it's black-eyed peas that bring luck and good fortune.

In Switzerland, dropping scoops of whipped cream on the floor symbolizes wealth in the upcoming year.

In areas of England, they drink wassail ("good health" in Gaelic) for a healthier year ahead.

In Spanish homes and central plazas, *las doce uvas de la suerte* ("the twelve grapes of luck") are eaten—one per month of the new year and one per strike of the clock at midnight on December 31. If you ever wonder how traditions like this get started, it is said the local practice was popularized broadly when grape growers had a bumper crop in 1909, and wanted the new year to be more prosperous (for them anyway, with a healthy uptick in grape sales).

# Happy New Year (continued)

IN JAPAN, TO PREPARE FOR THE RENEWAL OF THE NEW year, people are supposed to forgive each other, homes are cleaned thoroughly, and some people have *Bonenkai*, or "Forget-the-year parties," to say *sayonara* to the problems of the past year and to prepare for a better year. To eradicate 108 types of human weakness, Buddhist temples will strike gongs 108 times.

Many cultures have old traditions that include loud noises (gun shots, drums, sirens, or church bells) to either scare off the demons and bad, or simply to signal farewell to the old and hello to the new and happy.

In contrast, in Bali, a Day of Silence or *Nyepi* commemorates the new year on the Balinese calendar. Meditation and fasting are also part of the Hindu celebration.

Your personal New Year could start on your birthday—or today. What "new" would you like to add to make it happier?

# Ladder of Life

The Pew Research Institute conducts Global Attitude Surveys, asking people around the world to pick a number between zero and ten to describe where they are on the Ladder of Life. Ten is tops for well-being.

From 2007 to 2014, the countries that had a dramatic increase in the percentage of people who scored themselves at seven or above include:

- Indonesia    + 35 percent
- China        + 26 percent
- Pakistan     + 22 percent
- Malaysia     + 20 percent
- Russia       + 20 percent
- Turkey       + 13 percent
- Chile        + 12 percent
- Peru         + 10 percent

Pew notes that economic growth increased feelings of well-being, but that it wasn't the only factor. Their results showed that people tended to value immaterial things—e.g., good health and a quality education—among the most important things in life.

What rung (one to ten) would you say you are on?

# Auspicious Symbols

THROUGHOUT THE HIMALAYAN ROYAL KINGDOM OF Bhutan, the eight auspicious signs are prevalent symbols of Buddhism, often part of artwork. They are a kind of ancient visual formula for a good and happy life in mortal form and beyond.

The eight symbols, called Ashtamangala (Sanskrit) or Tashi Dagay (Dzongkha, the Bhutanese language), are in temples, classrooms, and fortresses, as well as on wall hangings and clothes. The lotus, conch shell, treasure vase, parasol, golden fish, endless knot, victory banner, and dharma wheel are symbols and can be seen as kinds of good fortune and happiness.

These emblems also show up as teaching tools and spiritual symbols in Hinduism and Jainism, sometimes with different interpretations.

The eight auspicious signs are:

- THE LOTUS is a spiritual symbol of compassion and purity, an icon for the spiritual unfolding and blossoming that can rise out of the murky waters of attachment.

- THE CONCH SHELL represents the blowing or blasting away of evil, and letting the good be heard to awaken people from ignorance. It stands for authority and power.

- THE TREASURE VASE stands for an abundance of treasures, long life, prosperity, and the infinite value of dharma.

- THE PARASOL protects from obstacles, disease, and harm. It is often related to wealth and royalty.

- THE GOLDEN FISH stands for happiness, prosperity, abundance, and fertility, and can be a metaphor for swimming fearlessly in the sea of life.

- THE ENDLESS KNOT has no beginning or end. It is representative of meditation and karma, and the Buddha's infinite wisdom and compassion. The image evokes the spiritual and the secular, intertwined.

- THE VICTORY BANNER waves for overcoming the earthly evils and for the Buddha's ultimate victory of enlightenment.

- THE DHARMA WHEEL is a symbol of the laws of Buddhism. The eight spokes represent the Noble Eightfold Path toward enlightenment.

Do you have symbols that represent and inspire elements of happiness for you?

# Gross National Happiness

IMAGINE A SMALL ROYAL KINGDOM UP IN THE HIMALAYAN mountains, nestled between India and China, but relatively closed off from foreigners—a kingdom where Buddhism has been prevalent for more than a thousand years, where waterfalls power prayer wheels, and there are no televisions, ATMs, or traffic lights.

When his Majesty the Fourth King of Bhutan Jigme Singye Wangchuck took over this land from his father in 1972, he wanted to retain his country's character but, at the same time, to allow it to experience the best of the modern world.

Most nations determine their "success" materially, by measuring Gross National Product (GNP—all the goods and services produced by the citizens of a country) or Gross Domestic Product (GDP—all the goods and services produced *within* a country).

The King of Bhutan, however, wanted to evaluate his country's progress and his people's well-being in a broader way than just economics, so he conceived of the Gross National Happiness (GNH) index as a gauge.

This small nation set new standards and, since then, other countries have been exploring how better to determine their own peoples' quality of life and happiness, not just their economic success.

In pioneering a Gross National Happiness Index, leaders in Bhutan had the daunting task of trying to figure out how to measure and track happiness and well-being. They developed a matrix to measure thirty-three factors under nine categories:

1. Psychological well-being
2. Standard of living
3. Good governance
4. Health
5. Education
6. Community vitality
7. Cultural diversity and resilience
8. Time use
9. Ecological diversity and resilience

What categories would you create for a GNH index to measure a nation's true "progress," not only economic success?

What matrix would you use to measure your own personal happiness?

# Moonrise

HAVE YOU EVER ENJOYED THE TIMELESS RITUAL OF watching the moonrise over the mountains? It's a moment of awe and "ah!" that makes one glad to be alive. Then, if you run farther back, and turn around, you can sometimes watch the moon elevate again from behind the mountain— the luminous sage rising large and majestically, a mega spotlight for earth and sky.

The moon connects us to all cultures all over the globe in all times, and even dangles the promise of a different lunar culture in the future. Men have walked on the moon, and the science and wonder continue. The moon also continues to choreograph the ocean's tides, in and out, all over the planet.

Breathing deeply while watching the moon can be a kind of moon meditation. The goal: to rise out of petty thoughts and simultaneously be bathed in a cosmic mystery of feeling very small and limitlessly connected to the grand.

# Defining

When asked "What is happiness?", artist Sergei Barantsev shares the poem "Epitaph" by Christopher Logue, which offers some answers that include "listening to the sound of a young girl singing down the road after she asked me the way."

In the Russian novel, *Monday Begins on Saturday*, by brothers Boris and Arkady Strugatsky, a graduate student is writing a dissertation for the Department of Linear Happiness. He refers to the "Epitaph" poem when he decries trying to define happiness. "Such things do not allow for algorithmizations," he claims. "Yet humans have been searching for definitions and formulae for happiness for millennia."

Ask several people today, "How would you define happiness?" What's your answer?

# "How Would You Define Happiness?"

Answers can be diverse:

*Maybe McFerrin's whistling to "Be Happy" as an opener? Kiimak ool = "Happy" in Mayan. Anyway… be happy. The alternative's not so hot.*

—Rob Rourke,
musician and landscape architect

*I believe the most apt definition of "happiness" would be: Absence of want in all its degrees.*

—Norman Dorff,
ninety-one-year-old retired businessman;
active humorist and happy-maker

Joel Shurkin, science journalist; co-winner, Pulitzer Prize, offered this:

*Too much of a good thing is—wonderful.*

—Mae West

*Three words: Honest, sincere, and earnest, in that order. This leads to a happy life.*

—Eloise Buckner, therapist

*Forgetting yourself.*

—Chris Gage, event engineer

*It's the state of mind in which one's health, prosperity, preparedness, and optimism meet spiritually with vision, compassion, purpose, and joy.*

—Stephanie Stokes Olive,
author liaison for Anguilla Jollification
Literary Festival

*I haven't found my definition yet.*

—Delroy Lake,
President of Anguilla Hotel
and Tourism Association

# Bluebird of Happiness

THE "BLUEBIRD OF HAPPINESS" IS A RECURRING THEME in twentieth-century popular culture. It was the title of a popular song in 1934.

In 1940, Shirley Temple and a fairy used magic to time travel to both the past and the future, seeking the bluebird of happiness in *The Blue Bird* (a remake of a classic 1918 silent film). Of course, they found happiness in neither place; it was in the gift of the present.

A few years later, the upbeat Disney song "Zip-a-Dee-Doo-Dah" (1946), included the lyrics "Mr. Bluebird's on my shoulder."

The idea of bluebirds as positive symbols, however, goes much further back.

Different Native American tribes had bluebirds in their stories, some associating them with the sun and others with spring—both life-affirming images.

During the Shang dynasty, which dates back to earlier than 1,000 B.C. in what is now China, the Qingniao (sometimes interpreted as a bluebird) was the messenger of the "Queen Mother of the West," who symbolized immortality and prosperity.

# "Happy as a Lark"

"Happy as a lark" is a phrase that suggests being extra happy and joyful.

The origin of the saying is unknown, but those who have heard a lark's melodious songs on a spring day can understand why the saying has survived. Chaucer and Shakespeare both wrote of larks singing at daybreak. In the stories of different cultures, larks serve as messengers to heaven or the gods.

Most birds only sing while sitting around (perching). Bill Thompson III, the editor of *Bird Watchers Digest*, notes that, "Many larks sing while hovering or flying, which might be the equivalent to whistling while you work."

Larks are also good at mimicking other birds' songs.

If you could fly, what would you sing?

# Magical Kingdom

*To all who come to this happy place: Welcome.*
*Disneyland is your land. Here age relives fond*
*memories of the past, and here youth may savor the*
*challenge and promise of the future.*

—Walter E. Disney,
July 17, 1955, at the opening of Disneyland

DISNEYLAND PARK IN CALIFORNIA IS BILLED AS "THE
Happiest Place on Earth" and has entertained more than
700 million visitors since it opened. It has broken records
for the largest accumulated total of guests of any theme
park in the world.

People from all over the world head to Disneyland,
for its entertaining fantasy and fairytale themes, as well
as a Tomorrowland. Many feel happiness in the magical
kingdom and theme park that were designed to help
people escape reality and reconnect to their inner child.
Disney overcame many obstacles to build the happy place
he envisioned, and today, multiple generations visit to
fondly enjoy their pasts or savor the promises of the future.

What about Disneyland can help happiness in your
land?

# It Began with a Mouse

WALT DISNEY, THE CREATOR OF THE "HAPPIEST PLACE ON
Earth," went bankrupt with his first animation studio, but
he didn't let that stop him from following his passions and
pursuing happiness. Disney went on to win twenty-two
Academy Awards for his films, to create Disneyland, and to
develop Walt Disney World in Florida.

Disney once said, "I only hope that we don't lose sight
of one thing—that it was all started by a mouse." Mickey
Mouse.

Our lives are filled with twists and turns, and we never
know how something little, like an animated mouse, might
make millions of people laugh and start an empire.

In 1934, after success with Mickey Mouse and other
series of shorts, Disney wanted to create his first animated
feature film. Both his wife and brother tried to talk him
out of it. The project was dubbed "Disney's Folly," and
it took four years to make. When the project ran out of
money, Disney had to borrow funds, but the end result was
wildly successful. That film was *Snow White and the Seven
Dwarfs*.

Of the seven dwarfs in the movie (Sneezy, Grumpy,
Sleepy, etc.), only one asks Snow White, "Who are you?"
That's Happy!

# Dhammapada Happiness

READING SOMETHING ILLUMINATING BEFORE MEDITATING
or going to sleep can clear the mind of destructive
thoughts. You may have your own collection of favorite
quotes from a religion or great thinker.

Much of the wisdom of Buddha was gathered in the
Dhammapada. *Dhamma* means "teachings" or "truths" and
*Padda* signifies "verses" or "path."

Buddha did not advocate that people follow him.
Instead, he recommended they question what they hear,
and seek a path of enlightenment away from attachments
to pain, greed, envy, jealousy, and illusions. For the Buddha,
and his followers, this was the path to true happiness.

Following are some excerpts about happiness from the
oral teachings of Buddha, twenty-six centuries ago.

*All that we are is the result of what we have thought: it is founded on our thoughts, it is made up of our thoughts. If a man speaks or acts with a pure thought, happiness follows him, like a shadow that never leaves him.*

—Verse 2

*For hatred does not cease by hatred at any time: hatred ceases by love, this is an old rule.*

—Verse 5

*He who seeking his own happiness does not punish or kill beings who also long for happiness, will find happiness after death.*

—Verse 132

*Do not speak harshly to anybody; those who are spoken to will answer thee in the same way. Angry speech is painful, blows for blows will touch thee.*

—Verse 133

*Rouse thyself! Do not be idle! Follow the law of virtue! The virtuous rests in bliss in this world and in the next.*

—Verse 168

# Wake Up!

WE READ ABOUT SPIRITUAL AWAKENING, BUT LITERALLY waking up is a daily occurrence that sets the course of what is to come. Do you have any morning rituals that enliven your gladness to be alive? Some ideas:

- If you can, set your alarm to play music that makes you happy, or set it to a show that makes you laugh.

- Try a few good stretches and deep breathing before you get out of bed.

- Try horizontal prayer, or meditation, or positive wake-up thoughts.

- Start a lovely tradition of saying positive things to your bedmate before you leave the bed…or just say "good morning" out loud to yourself, and then "make it so."

# Wireless Makeover

YOUR PHYSICAL DEVICES THAT CONNECT YOU WIRELESSLY with the outer world could also help you to be connected wirelessly within for more joy.

What images make you happy? A photo of a child you love? A gorgeous mountain? A funny dog or cat?

You can change what your computer screen shows or change the wallpaper or background image on your mobile devices. Choose a visual that triggers a smile in you and anyone who sees it. You can change it often. Try a fantastic photo of the fish you snorkeled with on your last vacation, or of someone you love laughing, or an image of something you do that you really enjoy.

Are there ringtones on your phone that make you laugh?

Does adding emoji or silly icons make you and your recipients cheerier?

Do you have great happiness quotes you could add to your signature for emails to share the insights? Or maybe you want to have jokes that make people laugh?

What else can you do to make your smart devices make smart tools that tickle your happiness and spread the well-being wealth?

You can be a cyber ambassador for more happiness in the world.

# Cyber-Seeking

In today's age, another way of seeking is to wander the World Wide Web.

Some ideas for your cyber-seeking:

- Try multiple search engines and put in "happy" or "happiness" and then whatever comes to your mind. Try "happy art" or "happiness bicycles" or "happy creativity." Try adding your favorite hobby or your next vacation destination.

- Seek out happy movies for your weekend or other books on happiness. Find a new song or video about happiness. Check out the happiness apps available for your phone.

- Research the latest studies on happiness from neuroscience experts, psychology whizzes, or governments exploring policy changes and medical trials. All kinds of findings could have emerged since this book was gathered.

- Create a list of bookmarks for your favorite happiness websites or any websites that help you to be happy. There are medical sites with happiness as a category now, offering ways to increase well-being and decrease depression. There are also happiness organizations.

- Go to your favorite social media outlets, or try new ones, and search with "happy" in mind. You may be inspired by photos, quotes, stories, and happy places, or you may connect with people who are happy. You may have your own material to add.

- Take a free online course. Over 200,000 people have registered for "The Science of Happiness," one of the many happy services offered by Berkeley's Greater Good Science Center.

# More Internet Ideas

### Happiness Folder

Create a happiness folder that lives on your desktop where you see it every day. Put in quotes you like. When you get an email or social media message that makes you happy, add it to your folder. Include compliments and "I Love Yous" if they make you smile, as well as inspiring stories about others. Add photos you like. Include articles that uplift you.

### Feed Yourself Happy

Some websites have free feeds or newsletters you can sign up for, so your inbox can add to your up mood. You can have almost anything arrive in your electronic devices—from jokes and uplifting, funny images of animals, to meditation and breathing exercises—to help you feel great. If you enjoy a hobby, you can probably get tips and tales sent to you automatically, too.

### CyberSupport

If you are trying to change habits for more happiness, you may be able to join a cyber support group or pick a real-life friend to communicate with. You can cheer each other on for more cheerfulness in your virtual and actual worlds.

# Enjoy the Show!

Enjoy the ballet. Head to the stadium. Take in a show.

People who enjoy cultural events are happier and healthier, according to research published in the *Journal of Epidemiology*. That includes men who enjoy ballet, art, and theater, as well as men who volunteer, engage in physical activities, and enjoy outdoor hobbies. The women in the study who rate the highest on happiness attend both church and sporting events.

Researchers admit they don't know whether happier people enjoy those kinds of activities, or if interacting with culture in those ways helps people be happier.

Since social interactions, learning, and exercise are all also associated with more happiness, you now have multiple reasons to get out there and enjoy the show.

# Itches

Ross Sonne, a happy eighty-six-year-old who laughs well, gave his definition of happiness with a smile. "At my age," he said, "happiness is being able to scratch where it itches."

There are so many kinds of itches.

Your brain is curious and twitchy to know. Happiness can be finding a fascinating answer or something else to make you curious. Learning is kind of like scratching an itch.

People have "wonder" lust (not wander)—a hunger to get another fix of beauty, awe, or delight. Happiness can be having the mobility, mindset, and working senses so you can feed that wonder.

You may be itching to see a good friend or family member.

And of course, there are times your skin simply itches, and doesn't it feel good and satisfying to be able to scratch?

# Happy Names

JOY, GAY, BLYTHE, BLISS, FELICITY, AND MERRY ARE ALL female names that connote happiness. Gwyneth means "happy, blessed" in Welsh, and Farrah translates as "happy" in Arabic. Allegra is Italian for "joyful." Helga harkens back in Scandinavian languages to mean "happy" and "blessed," and sometimes "holy."

The name Hilary comes from the Latin word "hilaris," originally meaning "good cheer" and evolved to mean "boisterously joyful." The words "hilarious" and "exhilarate" use the same root word.

Carol, Caroline, and Carole can all mean "happy song," going back to French origins. Edith means "happy" from older English, and Beatrix can mean "bringer of joy" in Latin.

The male name Felix means "happy" or "lucky" in Latin, Edwin means "happy friend" and Asher is a male name meaning "happy" or "blessed" in Hebrew.

# Happy Party

Host a Happiness Dinner Party. Ask guests to wear colors that make them the happiest. And let the table fare be full of potluck pleasures: Ask them to bring a food or drink that makes them happy.

For those who also want a cinema soirée, ask friends to think of a scene from a favorite movie that picks up their mood. The after-dinner entertainment can be people sitting around today's "campfire"—the flat-screen TV—to talk about their scenes and explain why they make them happy. You may learn about your friends, and about new movies that could make you laugh or learn.

Do you remember the classic film *Groundhog Day?* The Bill Murray character keeps reliving the same day until he finally gets it right—and rescues cats and people and shares his talents and heart with others. In the process, he transforms from a miserable self-centered guy who collects proof of the world's failures, into a charming human who makes those around him happier. He then attracts the love he wants to give and to get.

What movie scene would you bring?

# Themes

BASKING IN THE COLLECTIVE CONTENTMENT OF BEING
with some of your favorite people may be party enough,
but here are some starter themes for something different:

**Sports Hi-Five** — Have guests wear the colors of "their"
team (any sport) and bring a video clip of a favorite sports
moment, where the human body transcends the ordinary.

**Go Literary** — Have guests bring passages that convey
happiness through characters, settings, or insights. Many
authors have created some choice quotes about happiness
that you could put at each place setting. Have guests pick
an author's name out of a hat and see what happens when
they try to match their authors with the quotes to find their
places at the table.

**Giving** — Ask guests to bring information about a favorite
cause. Let them talk for a couple of minutes about why they
champion certain nonprofit efforts. At the table, have them
feel under their chairs to find a Charity Check (donations
that can be given to any charity the guest chooses) taped
beneath them. Depending on your finances, each of your
guests or one lucky one could enjoy the joy of giving,
thanks to you.

# Naps

*There is more refreshment and stimulation in a nap, even of the briefest, than in all the alcohol ever distilled.*

—Ovid, Roman poet, first century

*I like to nap. I do like to sleep. Sometimes I sleep in between takes.*

—Jodie Foster, actress, twenty-first century

LEONARDO DA VINCI, GENE AUTRY, AND ELEANOR Roosevelt all relied on naps to be at their best.

Naps were so vital to his life, Winston Churchill kept a bed in the House of Parliament. President Kennedy and his wife, Jackie, would have the drapes drawn after lunch for some naptime. Jackie reportedly convinced the next president, too, that naps make a vital difference.

President Johnson would actually change into his pajamas for an afternoon nap, then wake to begin his "second shift" of the day. President Reagan joked that his chair should be inscribed "Ronald Reagan slept here." Inventor Thomas Edison would take naps anywhere—on a bench or in a closet—and could fall asleep instantly.

These days, the National Sleep Foundation recommends naps of twenty to thirty minutes for "improved alertness and performance," even for folks who aren't inventors and world leaders.

# Z Instead of ZZZs

*You have merely to let yourself be progressively*
*invaded by serene afternoon sleep, like the spiritual*
*drop of anisette rising on the sugar cube of your soul.*
                                                    —Salvador Dalí

IN HIS *FIFTY SECRETS OF MAGIC CRAFTSMANSHIP*, THE
pioneering painter Salvador Dalí shares his secrets for a
mini-nap that he claims catalyzed his creativity. To make
sure he did not oversleep, he would sit in a hard armchair,
lean his head back, and rest his arms with his hands hanging
in space. Between his thumb and forefinger, he would hold a
heavy key over an upside-down plate on the floor.

When he relaxed enough, his hand would drop the key,
and the clatter would startle him awake with new creative
ideas.

He claimed he learned of less-than-a-minute napping
from the Capuchin monks of Toledo.

Reportedly, Aristotle and Einstein also took mini-naps
that could induce a hypnagognic state (transitioning from
awake to asleep), possibly unleashing a fluidity of creative
and inventive thought. This threshold of consciousness has
also been called "lucid dreaming."

Maybe trying a "Z" instead of "ZZZZs" will unlock some
happy creativity for you.

# Happy Factors

THE AMERICAN ASSOCIATION OF RETIRED PERSONS (AARP) decided it was time to "create a more robust understanding of what Happiness and Well-being mean to middle-aged and older Americans." So, in 2012, it conducted a survey of more than four thousand people between the ages of thirty-five and eighty. AARP discovered that most Americans ages thirty-five and up are happy, but the numbers were at their lowest level ever, and dropping (possibly due to the economy at the time).

The AARP survey asked people to classify themselves as very happy, pretty happy, or not too happy. African Americans had the highest percentage of respondents in the top category (24 percent), and Hispanics came in a close second (23 percent). Hispanics also came in second in the bottom group, with 26 percent reporting that they are not-too-happy. Asians had a higher percentage of not too happy people (32 percent) .

Among its findings, the AARP study confirmed what grandparents have been saying for years: Without your health, you have a much lower chance of being happy; and money can't buy happiness, but it helps.

AARP's SURVEY IDENTIFIED A U-SHAPED HAPPINESS CURVE, with people in their early fifties the least happy. Later in life, after retirement, people have more time to enjoy life. The person most likely to be the happiest, according to a combination of all the findings, is a highly educated, married woman who is retired.

In its survey, people were asked to identify things that add to their personal happiness, and the top two answers were "kissing or hugging someone you love" (72 percent) and "watching your children, grandchildren, or close relative succeed" (72 percent). Those two beat out spending time with family or friends (69 percent), having an important prayer answered (56 percent), and making progress on personal goals (51 percent). Playing card, board, or video games came in last (15 percent).

Pets contribute "a lot" to most people's happiness (57 percent). The number was considerably higher for women aged sixty-six to eighty (81 percent) and lowest for men aged thirty-five to forty-five (42 percent).

# Spell It Out

IN ADDITION TO DOING THE RESEARCH, COMPILING THE data, and telling you how to be happy, some people spell it out for you, too.

Dr. Martin Seligman, director of the Positive Psychology Center at the University of Pennsylvania, advocates PERMA—an acronym for five main elements for developing and measuring well-being. The Center runs an Authentic Happiness website and defines *positive psychology* as "the scientific study of the strengths that enable individuals and communities to thrive."

Seligman is also leading a multimillion-dollar study into positive medicine, looking at health assets instead of risk factors. This is not unlike the way he and others look for positive elements in psychology, instead of the older disease model where the focus was on disorders and unhappiness.

PERMA
**P**ositive Emotion
**E**ngagement
**R**elationships
**M**eaning
**A**ccomplishment

THE ACRONYM "GREAT DREAM," IS COMPOSED OF THE TEN Keys to Happier Living (see below), based on the latest research according to Action for Happiness, a movement and website for "people committed to creating a happier and more caring society." Their patron is the Dali Lama.

Action for Happiness maintains that 50 percent of happiness is genetic and upbringing, 10 percent is income and environment, and 40 percent is activities and relationships. It offers exercises for people who want to make those percentages add up to greater happiness by making better decisions in the areas over which they have some control.

GREAT DREAM
**G**iving
**R**elating
**E**xercising
**A**ppreciating
**T**rying Out
**D**irection
**R**esilience
**E**motion
**A**cceptance
**M**eaning

# Natural

*If the day and night be such that you greet them with joy, and life emits a fragrance like flowers and sweet-scented herbs, is more elastic, more immortal—that is your success. All nature is your congratulation, and you have cause momentarily to bless yourself.*

—Henry David Thoreau, *Walden*

SAVOR THE TREES AND SKIES THAT ARE YOUR NEIGHBORS where you live. Greet your garden's dawn with your senses, and salute the stars before you sleep.

Head to your local mountains, deserts, or beaches. Lie on your back, lift up your legs, and let your toes tease the stars or clouds. Laugh at the exuberance of a sunrise.

Pack up your pals and head to a national park. Be showered by a waterfall and wowed by a bear. Hug a tree. Smell infinity.

Enjoy natural happiness in nature. Congratulations!

# Aloha

WHAT IS HAPPINESS TO GREGORY SOLATORIO, A MAN WHO lives in a lush valley between a dramatically beautiful beach and a 250-foot cascading waterfall on the island of Moloka'i in Hawaii? And how would the same man define happiness when his calling is to be the "cultural practitioner" who keeps alive the traditions of his family that go back fifty generations in this fertile Halawa Valley?

Solatorio answers that happiness is "Aloha kekahi i kekahi"—a Hawaiian phrase that means, essentially, "love one another." The word *aloha* means both "welcome" and "love." This philosophy of loving one another also embraces loving the land—taking care of it and letting it take care of loved ones.

When visitors come to the Valley, locals greet them with a *honi*—touching their foreheads and noses with their guests' foreheads and noses . Each person breathes in or inspires the other's heart energy, then kisses on the cheek. The Solatorio family then shares their vision of happiness— Aloha kekahi i kekahi.

# I Flower

*Flowers always make people better, happier, and more helpful; they are sunshine, food, and medicine for the soul.*

—Luther Burbank, botanist

FLOWERS IN OFFICES CAN BOOST PRODUCTIVITY AND WELL-being. Flowers at home—on the table or in the garden—can bring smiles. People give flowers with get-well wishes, congratulations, sympathy—all aimed at helping people celebrate or feel better.

Flowers appeal to the senses of touch, smell, and sight, and they also engage the spirit. They can change the mood, so enjoy giving them to yourself or others. Savor garden strolls and discoveries in wild spring meadows.

How can we be like flowers for more happiness? The word "flourish" roots back to the Latin *flōreō*, meaning "bloom," "abound," "bright," "flowers," and to *flos* for "flower."

*The earth laughs in flowers.*

—Ralph Waldo Emerson

# Thank-You Notes

THANK-YOU NOTES ARE WRITTEN FOR BIRTHDAY GIFTS AND dinner parties. What about thanking people for life-changing help? Who would be on your list of people to thank if you thought of all the people who have made your life better?

Have you thanked the person who introduced you to the love of your life? Who helped you learn to read? Or who helped get you into college? Who makes you laugh the most these days? Try writing a thank you!

Research shows that expressing gratitude in thank-you notes can have a positive effect on your well-being for weeks after you write the note.

And the amazing potency of appreciation? This afterglow from written thanks is present even if you don't mail the letter or press "send" on the computer, according to research. Other studies have also shown that expressing gratitude is an important component of a healthy and happy life.

You could say that for a happy life, the best Rx is Thx.

A final note: Thank You for reading this.

# Dandelion—Weed or Wonder?

HAPPINESS IS OFTEN IN ONE'S PERSPECTIVE, AND THE dandelion shows how something can be good or bad, depending on your point of view and beliefs.

Although they are viewed as a weed by many gardeners and farmers in North America today, for most of human history in many cultures dandelions have been a source of food and medicine.

Dandelions can actually be good for many gardens. Below the surface, their roots can add minerals to the soil, as well as draw up water, making them helpful to nearby plants with shallow roots. Above the ground, dandelions can be food for butterflies and bees and other pollinating creatures.

Someday, tires may even be made from a type of dandelion that produces latex. And there's a rich legacy of superstitions about blowing the white seed head of the dandelion—from predicting when you will get married to granting your wish.

What do you currently see as a weed in your life that might be very beneficial to you if seen from another perspective?

# Nature

*There is pleasure in the pathless woods,*
*There is rapture in the lonely shore,*
*There is society where none intrudes,*
*By the deep sea, and music in its roar,*
*I love not Man the less, but Nature more.*

—Lord Byron,
"Childe Harold's Pilgrimage"

WHERE ARE YOUR HAPPY PLACES IN NATURE?

Can you close your eyes and feel better just imagining them?

Can you go now and sit under the planets, or a sheltering tree, or make plans to go immerse yourself in nature soon to enjoy your own happy nature?

When you travel, do you take time to seek the natural wonders of a foreign land, away from other travelers?

The Japanese have their own trips for a walk among trees, or "forest bathing" (*Shinrin yoku*), in dozens of designated forests. Their studies show positive effects on the nervous system with decreased anger, depression, and anxiety. A walk in the woods can do wonders.

# Star Compass

THE ANCIENT POLYNESIANS WERE "WAYFINDERS" WHO USED the heavens to navigate very long distances on the open seas in their double-hulled canoes. They relied on celestial navigation—the compass of the stars—to find new lands and to travel back home again.

Today, with GPS and satellite photos available at our fingertips, we don't need the stars to guide us to new places and back again. Still, we can use the stars metaphorically, to help us explore and to find our way home to ourselves.

Try it. Take some quiet time to lie on your back and watch the heavens. For many, the first impulse is to feel small in comparison to the vastness above. Instead, let your problems feel small and fleeting in the expanse of time and space. Watch your worries shrink as you set them next to the giant wonders of the universe. Let yourself feel like a beautiful expansive part of the majesty of the cosmos... because you are!

# Brightest Star

THE POLYNESIANS USED THE BRIGHTEST STAR IN THE SKY AS a key guide for their travels in the Southern Hemisphere. The star was given many names by different Polynesian groups, who used it as a key marker for finding the latitude of Fiji. It was also a part of Manu, the Polynesian Great Bird constellation.

To the ancient Greeks and Romans, that bright guide was the Dog Star, part of the constellation of Canis Major (Greater Dog). Today, that star is known to most westerners as Sirius (Greek for "glowing").

Many cultures made up stories about constellations and gave them names. When looking at the stars in your skies, you can do the same. Watching the stars unrushed, you may even feel a deep sense of gratitude and appreciation that feeds your happiness. What stories can you imagine that support your happiness? How can the stars help tell those stories and guide your voyages in life?

# Keep On Swimming

*I have swum for hours across distant oceans, and
I have watched the sunrise turn the sea into liquid
gold, red, and orange. I have walked in moonlight
through foreign cities and towns. I have loved and
been loved. I have seen the seasons subtly change
and watched myself grow and learn as the earth
has moved closer to and then away from the sun.
I have felt a deep connection to nature, to people,
and to life.*

*These memories bring me great happiness. I think
a life that is well-lived gives one great happiness.
It is the doing of what you love, being with the
people and animals that you love, and sharing good
times—this is what brings happiness. Love of life,
of oneself, and of other people brings the greatest
happiness.*

—Lynne Cox

LYNNE COX IS AN INSPIRATIONAL SPEAKER, A *NEW YORK
Times* best-selling author, and an International Hall of
Fame swimmer. She has fifty-eight open-water records in
seas and lakes around the world, including Antarctica, the
Bering Strait, the Straits of Magellan, Lake Titicaca, and
the English Channel. Her first record was as a teenager
swimming to Catalina Island, off the California coast.

# Zest

*True happiness comes from the joy of deeds well
done, the zest of creating things new.*
                              —Antoine de Saint-Exupéry

NO ONE ELSE HAS YOUR COMBINATION OF TALENT, SKILLS,
ideas, and experiences. Using that personal fodder well can
generate purpose and happiness for you and for others.

Every day presents opportunities for "deeds well
done." Whether they are little daily chores, kindnesses to
others, or important parts of bigger arcs of your life, you
can enjoy the joy of deeds well done.

The joys of creating can be in everyday creativity.
It may be in explaining something in a new way to a
coworker or family member, finding an unusual solution
to a mundane problem, or simply seeing things differently
than you have before. You may recycle materials to let them
have new use, or connect two seemingly disparate ideas for
a positive outcome.

You don't have to be a world-class inventor or artist
to let your own unique package of traits enjoy the zest of
creating new things.

# Happy Places

Do you have a happy place you can go to? Is it in your mind? Or is it an actual place you can visit? If you don't, maybe you could find or develop one.

Mentally, you can be creative. Maybe your happy place is next to a waterfall of chocolate with hammocks that massage and play music, or a comfy compound in a massive banyan tree where everyone you love lives together.

In actuality, it's good to have physical places that you know engender a happiness, too—a park at the beach, or a friend's garden, or a favorite chair near a window, or a meditation and prayer niche, or your table at a restaurant, or_____?

Then, do you make time to enjoy your happy places?

Ideally every place can be happy for you, because you carry your happiness wherever you go.

*Athens is a good place—but happiness is much better; to be free from passions, free from disturbance.*

—Epictetus,
Greek philosopher (55-135 A.D.)

Want to go to some real "Happy" places?

Happy, in northern Texas, extols the motto "the Town Without a Frown." According to western lore, back in the 1800s, some cowboys were on an arduous and dusty cattle drive. They were delighted to find water and called the liquid bonanza "Happy Draw." The name for the nearby town that developed was obvious. Happy now has less than seven hundred residents, and no hotel for those who only want to dabble in Happy. The community *does* have a Happy Bank and Happy High School.

Happy Camp on the Klamath River in Siskiyou County, California, got its name during the Gold Rush boom. The story goes that when two prospectors arrived there, back in the early 1880s, one exclaimed, "This is the happiest day of my life." Now Happy Camp tags itself "the Gateway to the Marbles" (meaning the Marble Mountains) for memorable hiking to lakes and fields.

Lore also has it that people like stealing signs from Happyland, Oklahoma, an unincorporated area of eateries. Happy Jack, part of Port Sulphur, Louisiana, is a place for folks who love fishing to be happy. Happy Valley in Tennessee has three Happy Valley schools.

# Pre-Vacations

Do you have a vacation trip planned? Are you picturing yourself skiing down a slope, ordering another pastry at a French café, or sleeping on a Caribbean beach?

What about shouting "hello" into the gorgeous Grand Canyon, seeing the Mayan pyramids, hanging out on Aunt Martha's porch, or lounging on a cruise?

Some Dutch research shows that your happiness may be improved not only while *on* a vacation, but you can also enjoy elevated happiness for many weeks, or even months, *before* a vacation trip. Is it the sweetness of anticipation? The idea of escape?

The happiness levels of folks who had vacations planned was higher than those who didn't have vacation travel on the horizon. The exception—no surprise—is the stressful period immediately before a trip, when you are trying to get everything done before leaving.

If you aren't in pre-vacation mode now, you might start planning some travels today. And if you do, don't forget to use the leverage of trip-planning to boost your happiness before you leave. Just looking at pictures of your future destination and researching what wonderful things you can do there can help take your mind off stressful situations.

# Post-Vacations

Did you know there's an *Official Journal of the International Society for Quality of Life Studies*? There are people out there who are very serious about finding out what makes you happy.

For example, the *Journal* reported on a research study of the connection between holidays and happiness. The study showed that post-trip happiness levels were not related to how long the vacation was. Perhaps that means taking several shorter trips would produce more smiles than taking one long one.

It also turned out that post-trip happiness didn't last as long as pre-trip happiness, as many returning travelers slammed back into work and responsibilities. Perhaps leaving a day or two on the back end of your trip before returning to work could help. Or maybe beginning to plan your next trip soon after your return would stretch out the bliss-time.

Whatever you are planning, keep in mind that those who reported having a very relaxed trip had the biggest and longest-lasting boost in happiness after the trip was over. What would a very relaxed trip be for you?

You may just want to sleep on the beaches of paradise, or...?

# Experiences

EXPERIENTIAL TRAVEL IS NOW A MODE OF VACATION WITH more meaning. People want to learn a new skill, like Moroccan cooking or Irish dancing, or to follow the paths of ancestors. They want to participate, not just observe; they want to contribute, not just consume. Volunteering while traveling is a way to up the happy ante. Helping others provides perspective on our own problems and gives us a sense of accomplishment.

"Money can't buy happiness," as the familiar saying goes, but it can certainly have a role in helping you invest in magnificent experiences. You may be able to quantify "stuff" more than memories, but the things that make us happy are often invisible and have no price tag:

- Standing at the base of a redwood tree that was alive in the times of Jesus, Mohammed, and Leonardo da Vinci

- Hearing a favorite musician perform live

- Paddling through the flying bits of glow in bioluminescent waters

- Dressing up for safari and going to a local zoo or aquarium

For those who don't have the funds to travel far, a staycation spent at home or nearby can still be designed around fantastic memorable experiences.

*I believe that true happiness is allowing yourself to experience all of life's emotions. Happiness comes from understanding and recognizing where fear, old hurts, and pain come from, and instead of ignoring it and distracting yourself from it, going right into the center of it and dealing with it because liberation and freedom are on the other side.*

—Kate Hudson,
Golden Globe-winning actress

Nobody is exempt from the trials of life, not movie stars, not great athletes, not the Joneses, not the brilliant or famous—and not even the very happy. There is a difference between facing fears and fixating on them.

What experiences can help your journey? Can your unhappy help build your bigger happy?

# More Water

*In one drop of water are found all the secrets of all the oceans; in one aspect of You are found all the aspects of existence.*

—Kahlil Gibran

OUR BODIES AND OUR PLANET ARE MOSTLY WATER.

The sounds of water can be soothing fare. Fountains have enriched human life for millennia. People seek waterfalls and waves, and use recordings of oceans and rain for aural therapy.

Showers and baths often do more than clean the body; they can help reset the mind and soul. Many spiritual rituals involve water for purifying.

Oceans, rivers, and ponds have a long history of providing solace, inspiration, and happiness. Rain is called "blessings" in many parts of the world.

For all times and cultures, $H_2O$ is a part of any formula for life. Don't deprive yourself. Drink up, jump in, sip, savor, help save, feel, taste, smell, hear, see, float, flow.

Thank the waters.

# Courage

SCOTT CASSELL FOUNDED THE UNDERSEA VOYAGER Project, and is an advocate for the ocean's health. His TV credits include shows on National Geographic, MTV, and the Discovery Channel. His job credits include undersea explorer, submersible pilot and innovator, diving medical technician instructor, US Navy Diving Supervisor, and Counterterrorism Combat Diver for Special Ops. Yet when he addresses the role of courage in defining happiness, he isn't only referring to his dangerous work. Courage is very personal, which is why he also describes himself as a happy fiancé.

> *Human Happiness depends upon the finest human trait. Courage. Not Love, not giving, not kindness. Courage allows humans to do things over and above what our preservation instincts dictate. To Love, a human must place him/her self into a fully vulnerable condition open to the worst of all injuries. A broken heart. Without Courage, a human cannot fully Love.*
>
> *For those that Love our sea...you are my heroes and I salute you.*
>
> —Scott Cassell

# Joy

Robert Schwabach, creator of "On Computers," the world's longest-running syndicated column on computers, says, "Happiness is being married to Joy." This simple profundity is a wonderful metaphor—and a good thing, since his wife's name is Joy.

Joy Schwabach, who partners with her husband on the column, is also continually testing advances in technology. When asked "What is happiness?" she commented:

> *For me, happiness is striking the right balance between things I should do and things I want to do. Happiness is being pleased with myself. I don't need others for that, but they can be like mirrors, showing me some wonderful aspect I'd forgotten I had. When I'm sad, or out of sorts, a visit with a friend puts everything in perspective.*
>
> *Just writing about it makes me happy. It reminds me that sometimes, when I've rushed into a solitary space after a room filled with friends, that quiet moment of acknowledgment, that stillness, is the best of all.*

# Because!

Why? Because.

Be Cause.

Give yourself purpose. Give yourself cause.

Try being a happiness ambassador—giving kindnesses and smiles.

Volunteer to contribute time and talent to something that helps others.

Go through your closet and kitchen and find things to donate to those who need them.

Send off a funny card to a friend who is going through a rough patch.

Mentor someone who wants some guidance.

Take some of your garden flowers to a neighbor who is housebound.

Why?

Because.

Be cause happiness.

You can *be cause* and effect.

# Austen Approach

*Let other pens dwell on guilt and misery. I quit such odious subjects as soon as I can, impatient to restore everybody.*

—Jane Austen

JANE AUSTEN, THE GREAT WRITER OF *PRIDE AND PREJUDICE* and *Emma*, opens chapter forty-eight of *Mansfield Park* by letting her readers know her story will not reside in sorrows. She also offers great insight into paths for happiness and unhappiness by giving a status report on two of the main characters: Fanny, who lets delight overcome distress, and Edmund, who broods in sorrows, past and future:

> *My Fanny, indeed, at this very time, I have the satisfaction of knowing, must have been happy in spite of everything. She must have been a happy creature in spite of all that she felt, or thought she felt, for the distress of those around her. She had sources of delight that must force their way.*
>
> *It is true that Edmund was very far from happy himself. He was suffering from disappointment and regret, grieving over what was, and wishing for what could never be.*

Do you seek delight or disappointment? A Fanny or Edmund approach?

# Glad Game

*I know. Let's Play the Glad Game*
                    —Eleanor H. Porter, *Pollyanna*

IN *POLLYANNA*, THE BEST-SELLING 1913 NOVEL, THE YOUNG girl Pollyanna has been hoping for a doll, but all that remains on Christmas Day in the missionary barrel is a pair of crutches. Her father creates the "Glad Game" to cheer her, and, instead of disappointment, Pollyanna is grateful she has legs and is *glad* not to need the crutches.

Pollyanna's optimism and resilience fortify her. Her happy, giving character helps her warm a cold aunt's heart and turn an entire town around.

The book became a children's classic and added a new word to the English language.

"Pollyanna" can refer to someone with irrepressible optimism—someone resourceful and compassionate, who finds whatever good there is in a situation. The same word, however, has also developed a negative connotation for someone who is naïve or in denial.

Given today's research evidence of the value of optimism, kindness, and gratitude, perhaps more people would benefit from playing the "Glad Game" to make a happier world for themselves. Pollyanna, as a good-hearted person who improves others' lives, would be a role model— and her name, only a positive word.

# Contagious

*Whoever is happy will make others happy, too.*
—Mark Twain

BE HAPPY FOR YOU—AND FOR OTHERS! MOODS CAN BE contagious. You've seen it, and studies are confirming it.

So make sure you hang out with the happiest people you know. Strive to contribute to a contagion of happiness yourself. Share your light and laughter.

Remember the adage "misery loves company"? So be careful if you hang out with others who are unhappy. It's one thing if you are there to show compassion and for listening, love, and laughter—that can engender happiness!

Similarly, you can also benefit from a situation in which you are there to help each other, to forgive, or to express yourselves in order to share and to learn.

However, if you are trying to "out-misery" each other in a group, or to see who is the biggest victim, you lose even if you win. Leave the misery behind.

Try "*merriment* loves company."

Be a Pollyanna. Spread happy germs!

# Make Merry

A COUPLE FROM IOWA WHO HAD BEEN MARRIED MORE
than sixty years went to the Mayo Clinic for a checkup.
Instead of twiddling their thumbs in the waiting area,
they started tinkling the ivories of a nearby piano. They
spontaneously sparked an entertaining scene that lifted the
spirits of those around—and touched complete strangers
who had never even been to the Mayo Clinic.

Both the tune and merry mood were catchy and went
viral, in a good way.

Someone videotaped their gleeful improv and put
it on the Internet. More than 10 million people have
watched Frances and Marlow Cowan stand at the piano
and strike chords, then trade places in a dancing duet at
the keyboard. Their pleasure at making music together
is infectious, and you can hear other patients and staff
laughing.

Whether you are in the Mayo Clinic, the mountains,
or on a merry-go-round, what are your opportunities to
improvise some contagious happiness?

# Duty of Delight

*There is no duty we so much underrate as the duty of being happy.*

—Robert Louis Stevenson

FAR FROM BEING LUXURIOUS, FRIVOLOUS, OR SUPERFICIAL, being happy—even in bad times—can be essential to help others through the dark. Your happiness can be an example to others, and something that radiates like light, because of you.

The word *duty* comes from a Middle English word meaning "debt," and so does the word due. Perhaps we owe happiness as a form of gratitude for what we have. Perhaps it is part of the rent we pay for being here. Or perhaps we are due happiness for being here.

Duty is a responsibility that can be an ability to respond. Many sages tout that happiness is about how you interpret or respond to other people, to your feelings and situations, to life's roller coaster.

It is not somebody else's duty to make you happy, but your being happy could help others be happy, too.

# Invest Words in You

WRITE NOW TO FEEL RIGHT—BOTH NOW AND LATER ABOUT your past, present, and future.

Journaling can bring joy. The words you write to keep stock of your daily life can also pay dividends of pleasure later, especially if you note what you appreciate.

Some research shows that those who keep diaries of their lives can gain pleasure in the future when they reread the entries. What might seem ordinary now could be viewed warmly later, maybe even as something extraordinary. Sometimes even the mundane and the minutiae of life can seem to have a little magic when looked back on.

Your Narrative: Another kind of writing that research shows can be valuable is writing the narrative of your own story. If you look back on your life, what you repeat to yourself and others as the defining moments may not best define you. Experts advise that you can rewrite your script to not only tell your story more happily, but to realize the strengths within you to genuinely *live* more happily. Byron Katie, who created a system called "The Work," offers free guidelines online to help you use the power of the pen (or keyboard) so your words work for you, not against you.

# Happiness: "Happy As a Clam"

THE SAYING "HAPPY AS A CLAM" GOES BACK TO THE 1630S and is believed to be a shorter version of the original "happy as a clam at high tide" or "happy as a clam in the mud at high tide." At low tide, clams are in danger of being dug up for dinner. At high tide, with the ocean swirling above, they are hidden away, safe and cozy.

The shorter version of the phrase was popular enough by 1848 to be included in John Russell Bartlett's *Dictionary of Americanisms: A Glossary of Words and Phrases Usually Regarded As Peculiar to the United States.*

# Happifying

BARTLETT'S DICTIONARY OF AMERICANISMS PORTRAYS SOME of the expressive originality of the United States in the mid-nineteenth century. Next to "happy as a clam" in its listings is "happify" and "happifying" (that is, "to make happy" and "making happy"). They were active expressions in the United States back then.

Are you happifying anyone today?

In 1849, in her first public address, social reformer Susan B. Anthony urged,

> *Now, Ladies, all we would do is to do all in our power, both individually and collectively, to harmonize and happify our Social system.*

She went on to say:

> *We must remember that we live not for self alone, and that we are accountable to the great Author of all, not only for our own actions, but for the influence which they may have upon those with whom we associate.*

# Instrument of Peace

*LORD, MAKE ME AN INSTRUMENT OF YOUR
PEACE;*

*Where there is hatred, let me sow love;*
*Where there is injury, pardon;*
*Where there is doubt, faith;*
*Where there is despair, hope;*
*Where there is darkness, light;*
*Where there is sadness, joy.*
*O Divine Master,*
*Grant that I may not so much seek to be
consoled as to console;*
*To be understood as to understand;*
*To be loved as to love;*
*For it is in giving that we receive,*
*It is in pardoning, that we are pardoned,*
*It is in dying that we are born to eternal life.*

THE CHRISTIAN PRAYER ON THE PAGE TO THE LEFT IS A prescription for happiness. Although it has been attributed to St. Francis of Assisi and is sometimes named after him, scholars say he never wrote it.

The prayer first appeared in the early twentieth century and has been widely used since. When Mother Teresa won the Nobel Peace Prize in 1979, she referred to it. She also added it to morning prayers at her Missionaries of Charity.

The same year, Margaret Thatcher tipped her hat to the prayer when she won the election and became the United Kingdom's first and only female Prime Minister.

In 1984, South African activist Archbishop Desmond Tutu also credited the prayer when he received the Nobel Peace Prize.

# Ha Ha Power

HA HA HA, HE HO HA!

Laughter not only is a *sign* of happiness, it can also *stimulate* happiness. Research is showing that the cause and effect arrows go both ways.

Not only that—the real and pretend can both help! When you fake a smile or laugh, studies show that your body still releases endorphins and other chemicals that can help you feel better, as if your smile and laugh were genuine. With laughter, it doesn't take long before the forced laughter becomes authentic laughter.

Try adding laughter to your singing in the shower or your commute. Start cracking up with a child or friend and see how long you can laugh together. Nice "tee-hee" laughter could get you going, but when is the last time you enjoyed deep, releasing, stomach-stretching, sucking-in-air, snorting, and bellowing laughter?

Laughter can be contagious, too, so you could be helping others around you while you feel better.

What new daily habit would be better than adding more laughter?

# Join the Club

*If you are not happy, act like a happy person, and
you will become one.*

—The Laughter Yoga Club

THE LAUGHTER YOGA MOVEMENT CLAIMS MORE THAN SIX
thousand clubs worldwide, with members who meet to
laugh voluntarily and to develop a childlike playfulness.
They enjoy the aerobics and mood-boosting benefits of
good, prolonged belly-laughing, as well as the in-person
social interactions that feed happiness deliciously for
so many. The clubs say membership is free, and age and
gender don't matter.

The Laughter Yoga Clubs motto, "fake it until you
make it," is based on scientific evidence that the body
doesn't differentiate between the real and the acted. Laugh,
they say, and the happy chemical flow begins. Combining
laughter with yogic breathing, the clubs say, helps mental
and physical health as well as spreading the sounds of
happiness!

Yoga Laughter offers free exercises for people who
want to laugh alone, as well as tips for forming your own
laughter club. It includes different kinds of laughs and
breathing you can practice together.

# The "In" You

*It's not the circumstances, but what our soul is made of that makes us happy.*
—Voltaire, *Philosophical Dictionary*

OVER THE COURSE OF HUMANKIND THERE SEEMS TO HAVE been a general trend in Western cultures about what people think are the sources of happiness—from external causes (e.g., the gods, good luck, and wonderful fortune) to internal elements with the implications that individuals have some control. Voltaire, a leading French thinker during the Enlightenment credited the soul.

Today, three centuries later, many scientists are saying that one's perceived level of happiness is determined at least 50 percent by genetics or inherited DNA—another mighty force that resides within.

Research is also finding that other different internal factors like attitude, emotions, and thoughts can be influenced, with changed habits, for more feelings of happiness. It seems that almost every month, more is being learned about both internal factors (from body chemistry to meditation) and the impact of external factors (food, environment, education, income).

What is your soul made of? How would you describe your happiness DNA? Do you have good luck or do you create it?

# Quality of the Day

*We must learn to reawaken and keep ourselves awake, not by mechanical aids, but by an infinite expectation of the dawn, which does not forsake us in our soundest sleep.*

*I know of no more encouraging fact than the unquestionable ability of man to elevate his life by a conscious endeavor. It is something to be able to paint a particular picture, or to carve a statue, and so to make a few objects beautiful; but it is far more glorious to carve and paint the very atmosphere and medium through which we look, which morally we can do.*

*To affect the quality of the day, that is the highest of arts.*

—Henry David Thoreau, *Walden*

# Framing

WHEN YOU TAKE A PICTURE, YOU DECIDE WHAT TO PUT IN the frame. Even after you've snapped the photo, you can crop the image you want to keep.

The panorama before your eyes may include beauty and ugliness. There's a rising sun awakening colors in the sky and grungy debris and trash on the beach. What do you mentally photograph to preserve?

All of life has good and bad, and part of happiness is accepting the whole vista, but you can also choose what to focus on. You also may choose to pick up the trash and document that action for a positive change that you accomplish. Or maybe, for whatever reasons, you can't or don't want to remove the trash—it's beautiful to you.

When it comes time to remember a scene or a day, you are the photographer. You can frame the beauty or the ugly from the same events whether they're at the beach, home, or work. You can take true and inspiring pictures with or without the trash.

Taking time each day to frame the moments of happiness does not deny the world's troubles. It contributes to your album (whether tangible or inside your mind) that shows the beauties and the good.

# Intent

THE NATURE OF YOUR INTENT CAN AFFECT THE NATURE OF your experience, according to a study in *The Journal of Positive Psychology*. People who listened to upbeat music with the intent to feel happier actually felt more up for the next two weeks than people who listened to the same music with the intent to relax.

You can do your own experiments with intent. What if you went into the next business meeting, or bus ride, or market trip with the intent to be happy? Or at least questioned what your intent is? What if you looked for ways to make the experience better?

What if instead of just perpetuating habits like turning on the TV and flipping through channels, reaching for the chips but not tasting them, going for a run as something routine, you first were mindful of your acts and feelings and set an intent to feel happier?

# Ode to Joy

Ludwig van Beethoven integrated his version of Friedrich Schiller's poem "Ode to Joy" in the last movement of his Ninth Symphony. It is the first example of a major symphony using human voices. When the symphony premiered in 1824, Beethoven conducted, despite being deaf.

ODE TO JOY

*Oh friends, not these sounds!*
*Let us instead strike up more pleasing*
*and more joyful ones!*
*Joy! Joy! Joy, beautiful spark of divinity,*
*Daughter from Elysium,*
*We enter, burning with fervour,*
*heavenly being, your sanctuary!*
*Your magic brings together*
*what fashion has sternly divided.*
*All men shall become brothers,*
*wherever your gentle wings hover.*
*Whoever has been lucky enough*
*to become a friend to a friend,*
*Whoever has found a beloved wife,*
*let him join our songs of praise!*
*Yes, and anyone who can call one soul*
*his own on this earth!*

*Any who cannot, let them slink away*
*from this gathering in tears!*
*Every creature drinks in joy*
*at nature's breast;*
*Good and Bad alike*
*follow her trail of roses.*
*She gives us kisses and wine,*
*a true friend, even in death;*
*Even the worm was given desire,*
*and the cherub stands before God.*
*Gladly, just as His suns hurtle*
*through the glorious universe,*
*So you, brothers, should run your course,*
*joyfully, like a conquering hero.*
*Be embraced, you millions!*
*This kiss is for the whole world!*
*Brothers, above the canopy of stars*
*must dwell a loving father.*
*Do you bow down before Him, you millions?*
*Do you sense your Creator, o world?*
*Seek Him above the canopy of stars!*
*He must dwell beyond the stars.*

# Ode to Joy (continued)

When the piece ended and Beethoven was turned around, the audience was standing up and waving handkerchiefs and hats so he could see their kudos. Beethoven's Ninth Symphony is one of the most performed symphonies in the world.

*Recommend virtue to your children; it alone, not money, can make them happy. I speak from experience.*

—Ludwig van Beethoven

# Debate

*All the happiness in the world stems from wanting others to be happy, and all the suffering in the world stems from wanting the self to be happy.*
                                                    —Shantideva

MARIANNE WILLIAMSON, AUTHOR OF FOUR *NEW YORK TIMES* best sellers, posted the above quote on social media, attributing it to Shantideva (Sanskrit for "peace diety"), an eighth-century Buddhist monk.

Responses to her post ranged from absolute agreement to vibrant protest. One side concurred that the path to happiness is others, not self; that giving is better than getting. On the other side, people pointed out that one cannot give what one does not have.

You need to develop your own happiness first, the protestors explained. Several shared how depleted they had been, or manipulated, trying to make others happy at their own expense. Once they, themselves, were happy, they said, they had power to help others be happy.

What formula do you use to find the right mix of happiness for others and for self?

# Settings

DO MODERN TECHNOLOGIES HELP OR HINDER YOU AS YOU try to start your day? A recent study showed that 63 percent of nineteen- to twenty-four-year-olds take their smartphones to bed, and 80 percent of that age group reach for those phones within the first fifteen minutes of waking up.

Perhaps you can arrange for your smartphone to start your day with a positive image, quote, or sound. Think of it as receiving your message to yourself before you respond to other people's messages. Perhaps you could have a happy stash of some preselected happy quotes and images so every morning you can send out an uplifting message. You can start your day cheering others!

Here are some other ideas to launch your day in the right direction:

- Preset the thermostat to make your room a good temperature by the time you wake.

- Set up some favorite sights and smells nearby to make reality more inviting.

- Open any curtains: Studies show that natural light helps happiness more than artificial light.

- Leave a glass of water handy, so the first thing you swallow for the day is good for you.

# Ice Cream

*My advice to you is not to inquire why or whither, but just enjoy your ice cream while it's on your plate.*
—Thornton Wilder

SAVORING THE GIFTS OF "NOW" IS ONE WAY NOT TO overthink happiness. Don't compare your dessert to others', or wonder if you should have ordered differently, or feel guilty or unworthy of the riches in front of you.

Don't let tricks of the mind interfere with your ability to appreciate what's on your plate. Wait too long, and the ice cream could melt.

Sometimes life is sweet! Dig in!

# Enjoy Now

*If only we'd stop trying to be happy, we could have a pretty good time.*

—Edith Wharton

IN ANCIENT GREECE, AROUND THE SIXTH CENTURY B.C., A slave named Aesop noticed that people tend to be dissatisfied with what they have if they think someone else has something better.

In a fable to highlight how that foible can interfere with happiness, Aesop tells of a dog that stole some meat from a butcher shop and ran off to the woods to enjoy his bounty.

Ultimately, the dog comes to a river, looks in, and sees his reflection. Thinking that the reflection is another dog with another piece of meat in its mouth, the dog on shore decides he would rather have that "other" piece of meat.

When the dog opens his mouth to snatch the prize from his reflection, the meat drops into the river. The dog had what he wanted before, but when he was afraid someone else had something better, he winds up with nothing.

# Invest

*Nothing pays better dividends than investing in your self.*

—James Kafadar

WE ARE EACH OUR OWN CFO (CHIEF FINANCIAL OFFICER) when it comes to spending our time, money, and additional resources. But too often we spend on things that have puny ROI (return of investment).

When we invest in our own assets—development, education, and health—the wealth of our dividends lets us not only survive, but thrive.

You love photography? Invest in a good camera.

You want to learn a language? Take a class.

Investing in ourselves by improving our physical and mental fitness—our knowledge, our skills, our strengths, and our abilities—may seem risky, but the returns on such investments can help us live more engaged lives and become better able to help others, to solve problems, and to enjoy life—all components of happy living.

Make the best possible personal portfolio for invaluable happiness.

# Money

It's often said that "you can't take it with you." According to research, however, there are fulfilling ways that money can contribute to happiness while you are here:

- Buying gifts for others or paying for their java or jam can give you more joy than spending the funds on yourself, according to psychologists at the University of British Columbia.

- Giving to charities is also money well spent for your happiness (as well as the beneficiaries'), especially if you give the funds directly to someone associated with the cause.

- Experiences, more than things, let money help happiness. Go for good memories more than material goods to feel good longer. Think vacations, events, classes.

- Be artful. Looking at paintings or going to the theater can trigger your feel-good chemicals. Use your money as a patron of the arts for more pleasure and inspiration.

- Participating in sports kicks in good feelings too, according to researchers from the United Kingdom. Gym classes, team sports, and sports activities are cost-effective ways to elevate natural highs and health.

# Outsource

MONEY CAN ALSO BUY YOU TIME TO SPEND BEING HAPPY.

You can't buy extra minutes to add to your day, but it is possible to hire someone else to do the things that take time away from your being happy.

Hiring people to do things you don't like is a valuable resource for happiness, if spent right, according to a Stanford University study. If you can afford it, outsource chores, help others be employed, and use the time for happiness.

A caveat for all this currency creativity: The money spent should be funds you have above and beyond your basic needs. Not surprisingly, debt does not contribute to happiness. In many studies, money worries are a strong stress factor inhibiting people's well-being.

Exercise the plasticity of your mind, not the plastic of your credit cards.

Giving to others, purchasing experiences, and outsourcing can be fulfilling without spending buckets of money. Make a gift, go to free art galleries, volunteer your time to a charity, and barter some of your services with someone else for chores.

# Time Management

*Time is what we want most, but what, alas! we use worst.*

—William Penn

TOO OFTEN, OUR TIME-MANAGEMENT SKILLS IN THE modern world focus on how to be better at multitasking in the present, and then pushing harder into the future. Looking back, one often finds more sighs of the weary undone than smiles of the worthy done.

Our to-dos may read like heavy "too many dues"—more like debts than assets. But if we manage time really well—reminiscing, not regretting (past), doing (present), and anticipating, not expecting (future)—time can manage to help us feel happy.

A different kind of time management can focus more on how "to be" rather than all that you have "to do."

How can you shift what you do about your past, present, and future to be happier? You can manage your time (yesterdays, todays, and tomorrows) to enrich your happiness.

Here are some suggestions for happier time management:

## Past

We are the authors of our life narrative. When you look back, collect defining moments that show your strengths, happy memories, personal triumphs, and places that please you. Try to be grateful for what you have been able to do and see, and for the people you have loved. Don't compare yourself to others; you will always have more and less than others. Dwelling on perceived failures, faults, regrets, and wrongs sucks out the joy and leaves you thirsty. Gratitude can quench and nourish.

## Present

Seeing the present as a gift and being in the now are clichés, yes, but there's good reason for them to have been repeated so often. Do not linger on yesterday's angst or tomorrow's worries—but today's gifts. Live this moment, now. Look up from these words, take a moment to enjoy your senses and being alive.

## Future

The unknown can be anxiety-inducing or exciting. It is unspent bounty. Choose the blocks from your past and present that you want to use to build a happy foundation for the future, and add some scaffolding that will lift up your joy. Feel the abundance of your assets and the life force that means you have a future!

# Don't Worry!

"Don't Worry, Be Happy" resounded around the world when it was released in 1988. Bobby McFerrin's song won the Grammy for Best Song that year, and it was the first a cappella piece to be number one on the Billboard charts. Since then, it has sold more than 20 million copies. The tune and concept became a kind of mantra, anthem, and philosophy for some—a soundtrack for getting through daily troubles.

Although the song fills the world with upbeat words, the phrase "Don't worry, be happy" is credited to a man who spent decades not speaking—by choice. Meher Baba was a spiritual leader and author born in 1894 to Zoroastrian parents in India. He taught involution, an inner path.

Don't worry—both singing *and* silence can bring you the harmonies of happiness.

# Hakuna Matata

THE PHRASE *HAKUNA MATATA* MEANS "NO TROUBLES, worries, or problems" in Swahili. A song by that title in the 1994 movie *The Lion King* popularized the African phrase in American culture. The song teaches the lion cub Simba to focus on the present instead of wallowing negatively in the past.

Like Simba in *The Lion King*, do you have things from your past that consume you with worry? Can you sing your own "Hakuna Matata" to be happier?

The translated phrase "no worries" also became a common part of American conversation, sometimes as a response to a mistake or an apology.

For some, the essence of happiness is "no worries." Sometimes, the phrase reflects the attitude that life is relatively trouble-free. Other times, it conveys the sense that problems are a part of life, and one's responses should be with acceptance, faith, or courage instead of energy spent on worry.

# Smiles

Smiles are contagious. And just smiling can make you feel better, whether the smile was automatic or deliberate.

Most people smile because they feel good. Well, you can try it the other way too. When you *want* to feel good, try smiling. The happy effects of a smile are even more powerful than chocolate, says more than one study, but some chocolate fans would smile and beg to differ.

The father of the theory of evolution, Charles Darwin, also explained the theory of "facial feedback response" in his revolutionary *Origin of Species*.

Modern research backs him up: We give a smile and receive one back. Often more than one.

# Artful Play

ALEXANDER CALDER NEVER SUBSCRIBED TO THE NOTION OF the miserable artist. He once told a reporter that he didn't have time to be sad. For him, working was "the state of mind. Elation." He is credited with inventing the mobile, and his diverse artwork has brought smiles worldwide and won him a Presidential Medal of Freedom. To the playwright Arthur Miller, "he seemed more like someone at play than an artist."

As a creative kid in Pasadena, California, Calder picked up wires and debris from the streets and trashcans to make jewelry for his sister's dolls. His imagination was further stimulated when his mother took him to the Rose Parade in 1907. The eight-year-old saw colorful fanfare and horses in chariot races. He and his sister then fashioned their own little chariots with matchboxes. Decades later, he became well known for his wiry three-dimensional circuses and the show he created around them.

What "debris" can you find to make "art" just for fun? Can you gather trash on a beach or hiking trail and put it together creatively? What would be playful for you, so you could enjoy the childlike happiness of making inanimate objects be toys of imagination?

# Happiness: Great Thinkers

*I know that it gives one great inner force, calmness, and happiness to communicate with such great thinkers as Socrates, Epictetus, Arnold, Parker.... They tell us about what is most important for humanity, about the meaning of life, and about virtue.... I would like to create a book....in which I could tell a person about his life, and about the Good Way of Life.*

—Leo Tolstoy, *A Calendar of Wisdom*

THE RENOWNED RUSSIAN WRITER LEO TOLSTOY SPENT decades gathering quotes and passages for the book he wanted to write, and added his own insights. Eventually, he published *A Calendar of Wisdom* and considered it his greatest contribution, more than his classic novels *War and Peace* and *Anna Karenina*. In this spiritual devotional, Tolstoy offered many insights he hoped would bring happiness to his readers.

Tolstoy's book was popular in his own lifetime, then banned for decades under Communist Russia. When it was finally reissued in 1995, it sold more than 300,000 copies.

Who are the great thinkers you admire who provide you with "inner force, calmness, and happiness"? Do you have a place where you put the quotes that guide and inspire you? When was the last time you went back and read them?

# Everything

*If you have a garden and a library, you have everything you need.*

—Marcus Tullius Cicero

READING IS A POWERFUL WAY TO TRANSPORT OUR MINDS, change our moods, and learn and teach—all vehicles toward a happier state. The amount of reading children are exposed to at home is one of the greatest indicators of how well they will do not only in school, but in life.

Gardens have long been sanctuaries and sources of renewal. One of the original Seven Wonders of the Ancient World was the Hanging Gardens of Babylon.

Cicero, the man who thought books and libraries were core sustenance, was a Roman who introduced Greek philosophy to others and influenced the development of European languages.

He lived from 106-43 B.C., but the rediscovery of his letters is credited with influencing the Renaissance and Enlightenment.

Are you ready now to have "everything you need" according to Cicero? Find a good book (what's that in your hand?) and head to a garden.

# Education

*Live as if you were to die tomorrow. Learn as if you were to live forever.*

—Mahatma Gandhi

HAPPINESS MAKES AN IMPORTANT DIFFERENCE IN education, according to a study conducted in the Washington, D.C. area and reported in the Harvard Graduate School of Education website.

Other findings from the research done with St. Andrew Episcopal students, grades K–12:

- Happiness can be predicted by students' quality of relationships with fellow students and teachers, and by satisfaction with the culture of the school.

- Intrinsic motivation (an internal drive) is associated with happiness for all grades. It is a combination of autonomy, mastery, and purpose.

- Extrinsic motivation (external factors such as rewards, praise, and avoidance of punishment) was associated with happiness for the youngest students in first to third grades.

Happiness is positively associated with higher GPA (Grade Point Average) for grades four to twelve. In this study, happiness and results on standardized tests were not related.

When asked what they thought promoted learning, "fun and enjoyment" ranked high.

At any age, learning new material and mastering new skills and understanding may contribute to happiness both in the learning process and afterward. These studies indicate that being happy can also help with learning.

# Sleep

YOU MAY SLEEP A THIRD OF YOUR LIFE, SO WHY NOT MAKE IT a happy time? Both the quantity (get enough!) and quality of your sleep are linked to happiness.

Millions of Americans watch TV from bed and fall asleep during who-knows-what violence or conflict. Others get into bed with something to read that isn't restful. Some lie in bed reliving parts of their day, playing courtroom dramas in their heads, defending or prosecuting themselves and others.

Why not direct your thoughts while lying down to the best, most wonderful things that happened since the last time you were in bed? Perhaps you and your bedmate could share something good that happened during the day before you turn off the lights.

Create a ritual to help you transition from your conscious world to sleep. You may decide to pray, meditate, journal, or stretch before bedtime.

Make sure your bedroom is a sanctuary for you. Your bed and pillow should be comforts—the way they feel, look, and smell.

Many beds can be adjusted to change firmness or position. If your bed had a mood setting that you could adjust before you went to sleep, what would it be?

# Slap Happy

JUST SAYING "SLAP HAPPY" MAKES YOU FEEL A LITTLE looser and carefree, but where did the phrase come from? Would you believe jazz, and boxing?

*Cassell's Dictionary of Slang* provides two meanings and two origins for this American phrase.

*Slap happy* as a noun comes from the jazz world during the 1940s and refers to a real jazz fan. It's thought to be related to the practice of "slapping the bass" while playing jazz.

*Slap happy* as an adjective means "cheery," even a little eccentric, and it goes back to the boxing rings of the 1930s, when fighters could literally get slapped senseless, until their brains were jumbled.

The evolution of the term can be seen in the Urban Dictionary, which gives the most common definition of this diverse phrase as being "very tired" or "sleep deprived," sometimes including "inane rambling, strange remarks, odd random behavior (such as giving oneself a wedgie), uncontrollable laughter at one's own jokes."

# Pacing

*A friend of mine has a house with a basketball court and a pool. The guys go over and play basketball; I lie by the pool and nap in the sun. That defines me. That's consistent with who I am. I don't pretend to play basketball because I wanna feel like one of the guys. I wanna lie in the sun and relax.*

—Ryan Seacrest

*Take quiet moments when you need them. Tell your friends that you need them and not to read so much into them. And if your friends don't understand, that's okay. The way that they deal with things and feel things is different than the way you do, and that is what makes you all so special.*

—Amy Poehler

NOT CAVING TO PEER PRESSURE WHEN YOU KNOW WHAT'S best for you is a great strength. You can be a better friend when you have taken good care of yourself.

*If a man does not keep pace with his companions,
perhaps it is because he hears a different drummer.
Let him step to the music which he hears, however
measured or far away. It is not important that
he should mature as soon as an apple tree or
oak. Shall he turn his spring into summer? If the
condition of things which we were made for is not
yet, what were any reality which we can substitute?
We will not be shipwrecked on a vain reality.*
                                    —Henry David Thoreau

WE EACH HAVE A DIFFERENT PACE AND DRUMBEAT FOR
happiness on our journey.

# Follow Your Bliss

*If you follow your bliss, you put yourself on a kind of track that has been there all the while, waiting for you, and the life that you ought to be living is the one you are living. Wherever you are—if you are following your bliss, you are enjoying that refreshment, that life within you, all the time.*

—Joseph Campbell

ACCORDING TO *THE POWER OF MYTH* BY JOSEPH CAMPBELL with Bill Moyers, the phrase "follow your bliss" was inspired by the Upanishads, ancient wisdom written in Sanskrit, which Campbell considered to be "the great spiritual language of the world."

*There are three terms that represent the brink, the jumping-off place to the ocean of transcendence: Sat-Chit-Ananda. The word* Sat *means "being".* Chit *means "consciousness".* Ananda *means "bliss" or "rapture".*

—Joseph Campbell

What does "following your bliss" mean to you?

# Getting vs. Knowing

**GETTING** WHAT YOU WANT IS EASY.
**KNOWING** WHAT YOU WANT IS HARD.

*All too often, we react to the latest "shiny thing" dangling before us—the newest gadget, a bigger house, the most recent job posting. We chase them the way dogs chase squirrels—by instinct rather than choice—without giving much thought to what it will be like if we actually "catch" them.*

*Before embarking on the chase, sit quietly and contemplate: Exactly where does that impulse in you to make a change originate? What is the void you are trying to fill? If you succeed in this chase, will the victory fill the void? In other words, is that job, that house, that gadget truly what you want?*

*If you have found something you really want, the pursuit will be less frantic, more deliberate. The goal will be clear, and the path toward achieving it will shimmer as if catching the morning sunlight.*

*Finding that path is work, but following that path is a joy. And the reward is sweeter and longer-lasting.*

*Just think, what would you do with that squirrel if you caught it?*

—Victor Dorff, possibilitator

# Biblical

ENDURING AND ENDEARING VERSES ABOUT HAPPINESS FOR
Judeo-Christian faiths are found in the Hebrew Bible, also
referred to as the Old Testament in the Christian Bibles.
The Bible is usually cited as the most read book in the
English language, with almost 4 billion copies printed over
time.

*Make a joyful noise unto the Lord, all ye lands.*

*Serve the Lord with gladness: come before his
presence with singing.*

*Know ye that the Lord he is God: it is he that
hath made us, and not we ourselves; we are his
people, and the sheep of his pasture.*

*Enter into his gates with thanksgiving, and into
his courts with praise: be thankful unto him, and
bless his name.*

*For the Lord is good; his mercy is everlasting;
and his truth endureth to all generations.*

–Psalms 100
(Translation from the King James Bible)

*Happy is the man that findeth wisdom, and the man that getteth understanding.*

*For the merchandise of it is better than the merchandise of silver, and the gain thereof than fine gold.*

*She is more precious than rubies: and all the things thou canst desire are not to be compared unto her.*

*Length of days is in her right hand; and in her left hand riches and honour.*

*Her ways are ways of pleasantness, and all her paths are peace.*

*She is a tree of life to them that lay hold upon her: and happy is every one that retaineth her.*

—Proverbs 3:13–18
(Translation from the King James Bible)

# Swami

*Happiness is God. What kind of happiness? Eternal
happiness; not temporary happiness.*
                                    —Swami Satchidananda

SWAMI SATCHIDANANDA WAS A SPIRITUAL LEADER AND
author from India who founded Integral Yoga. Weeks after
he presented in Carnegie Hall in Manhattan, he opened the
famous Woodstock Festival in 1969. He told the multitudes
at Woodstock that "America is helping everybody in the
material field, but the time has come for America to help
the whole world with spirituality."

Although he had taught yoga and other Hindu and
Buddhist traditions, he believed all religions can lead
to the same universal God that is lasting happiness, not
momentary pleasures. His motto was "easeful, peaceful,
useful."

# Overcome

*It all comes to this: the simplest way to be happy is to do good. This is instant and infallible happiness. The surest proof that this is the law of cause and effect is, we may try every other conceivable way of being happy, and they will all fail. We cannot gather figs from thorns or grapes from thistles.*

—Helen Keller

*The best remedy for those who are afraid, lonely, or unhappy is to go outside, somewhere where they can be quite alone with heavens, nature, and God. Because only then does one feel that all is as it should be.*

—Anne Frank

BOTH OF THESE INSPIRING PEOPLE SHARED PATHS TO happiness for all despite their own terrible obstacles.

Anne Frank was a young Jewish teenage girl who kept a daily diary while hiding from the Nazis with her family during World War II. She coped with the ugliness by seeking the beauty. She died in a concentration camp but her incredible optimism lives on.

Helen Keller was both blind and deaf. Her world might have seemed dark and quiet compared to other people's but she didn't let it be limited or limiting.

# Remember

*People will forget what you said, people will forget what you did, but people will never forget how you made them feel.*

—Maya Angelou

## WHAT CAN YOU DO TODAY TO HELP OTHERS FEEL HAPPIER?

- Smile, or hug, or do both—depending on your relationship.

- Practice thoughtful kindness, saying or doing things you know will be well received.

- Bring up a happy memory you both share.

- Say something to generate a warm laughter that envelops you both.

- Say thank you for something specific that you appreciate.

- Mention something you truly admire about the person.

- Plan something the person would love, so you can both enjoy the idea and the anticipation, as well as the event when it occurs.

What you do today can help someone feel better now, and you can both enjoy happy memories in the future.

# Sun and Moon Light

THE SUN, LIKE ALL STARS, IS A FURNACE OF ENERGY, generating light and heat. The light from our sun gives us life on our Earth. Photosynthesis fuels plants, and the heat from the sun creates the water cycles of evaporation and nourishing rain.

No doubt, you know people who are like the sun—sending out rays of life, light, and warmth. Other people tend to orbit around this sustaining force.

The moon is actually a giant rock circling the Earth. The moonlight that illuminates the dark night is actually reflected light from the sun. The moon's proximity to Earth also allows it a force of gravity that makes the ocean's tides go in and out like liquid breath.

There are also people who, like the moon, are rock-solid and a positive force, though they may not be the center of the universe. They are good at reflecting others good light, and they don't mind orbiting around someone else if it provides beauty and luminosity.

Are you a sun or a moon? Do you generate or reflect light? Both modes are ways of promoting the happiness of others and making life brighter by day—and by night.

# Cultural

ADD SOME ARTS TO THE ART OF HAPPINESS—FOR MORE
happiness. Enjoy a symphony or a Madonna concert.
Be impressed with Impressionists.

That's what a Norwegian study with more than fifty
thousand participants concluded. The participants rated
themselves in four categories: their levels of low-anxiety
and low-depression, as well as their states of health and
"satisfaction of life"—a presumed combo for happiness.

Participants then noted how many cultural events
they attended that were receptive (passive) and active.
Receptive events included concerts, museums, exhibits,
and the theater. Active events referred to singing, dancing,
social clubs, and cultural activities that are outdoors.

People who included culture in their lives rated better
in all four categories, and the more culture they got the
better the ratings. The study indicated that women derived
even more benefits from active events than receptive
ones. Men benefited more from receptive events for their
happiness index.

Enjoy the arts of happiness!

# Eat Up

*Let food be thy medicine and medicine be thy food.*
*—Hippocrates*

SOME PEOPLE SWEAR BY THE POWER OF CHOCOLATE TO feel good. Others promote carbohydrates for comfort. A study shows that people who eat more fruits and vegetables are happier than other people. Amino acids in some hard cheeses are credited with reducing stress.

While there doesn't seem to be universal agreement yet on which foods could help everybody for happiness, nobody seems to deny that food choices can affect how you function and feel. Whether it's a smell that reminds you of your beloved grandma's cooking, or the taste of bliss you get from biting into something utterly scrumptious, food can be a core source of pleasure.

Make a list of what foods you can soar with and savor—without a sugar crash or guilt marathon. Keep some of your positive foods handy for when you want to ingest and digest happily, or share the bounty with others.

# Meals

*You learn a lot about someone when you share a
meal together.*

—Anthony Bourdain

STUDIES SHOW THAT COUPLES AND FAMILIES THAT TAKE
time to eat together (without the distractions of television
or other electronic devices) have stronger bonds and report
being happier. How can you incorporate more meals that
are face-to-face in your life?

Have you tried eating with work colleagues when
someone suggested a "no screens while we eat" approach?
You might be surprised what kinds of ideas cross pollinate
or how much you can laugh together when you take time
to talk to those with you instead of texting those who aren't
there.

# More Than 1,000 Opportunities

EVERY MEAL CAN BE AN OPPORTUNITY FOR MINDFUL eating—really paying attention and being grateful for what you eat, what you have, and where you are.

Or each meal can be a time to appreciate who you are with—for social interaction, the love of friends and family—nourishing far more than just your body and the bodies at the table.

Both approaches can "feed" happiness in daily and long-term life. If you eat three meals a day, that's 1,095 opportunities a year.

Try saying a prayer or setting an intent before the meal—even before preparing the meal.

Try engaging your senses and really tasting, feeling, smelling, seeing the food. Or try really seeing and hearing the people you are with, as well as enjoying the food and your setting.

Instead of "garbage in, garbage out" for your essence, think, too, of what foods and grace you consume and how you eat.

Bon appétit!

# Happy News Meal

IMAGINE IF YOU CREATED A NEW TRADITION TO HAVE A "happy news" meal at pre-determined times. The only permitted conversations are about the wonderful and positive things that happened during the day or the week, and only nice things can be said about the people and places that are mentioned.

Talk can be about the mundane—how shiny the silver looked when polished or how resilient the dandelion is that grew up through the cement cracks of the sidewalk. Conversation can tackle current-event issues in the world, but only if the speaker is expressing a positive view—for example, that a new bill was passed to fund education, that a new national park has opened, or that peace talks are progressing.

You may be surprised how hard it is for some people not to add negative commentary, to gossip, or to judge.

PICK A REGULAR NIGHT EACH WEEK FOR A HAPPY NEWS meal at home or with friends. Setting it on Tuesdays or Wednesdays might help you overcome any midweek slump.

You may find yourself spending the week collecting positive anecdotes from work or school, so you will have something to contribute to the next happy news conversation. Seeing what others choose to discuss may also provide some insight into what makes them happy.

One approach to keep the conversation positive might be to put a jar in the middle of the table. Each time someone slips up and says something negative, you can "put a lid on it" after the offender puts some money in the jar. You may agree ahead of time on a charity that will receive the funds when the jar is full.

Whether you try this at a family meal or with friends at lunch, note how it changes what you and the others talk about, and how you perceive your life.

# Don't Judge

SEND YOUR JUDGE AND JURY PACKING. LEAVE SUPERIOR attitudes and interpretations to the trained folks who wear robes in courts. Most of your judgments about yourself and others can stir up comparisons, resentments, anger...and you could be sentencing yourself and others to a term of unhappiness.

Are you so insecure that you need to be right at the price of making someone wrong? Are you so hard on yourself that you forget that mistakes are part of growth (if you learn from them instead of hurting yourself further)? You can learn from others' mistakes, too, and put your energy into your improvement, not condemning others.

They say if you are criticizing another for something, you should look in the mirror and see if the fault that bothers you is actually yours.

Can you look in the mirror and be honest and kind to yourself—observe but don't pass judgment and sentence? If you want things to change, kindly try change yourself first. Focusing on others' faults that you can't control is not a recipe for happiness.

How long can you go looking for solutions, not blame or fault?

# The Happiest?

DENMARK, HOME OF THE HAPPINESS RESEARCH INSTITUTE, consistently ranks at or near the top of Western studies based on self-reported "life satisfaction." And retired Danish women are the happiest of all, according to Eurostat's study. Of course, we can't all be retired Danish women, but maybe we can learn from their happiness:

- Researchers speculate that the older generation is happier because older people tend to know what makes them happy and don't care as much about what others think and expect. They are in more of a savor mode than a search or impress mode.

- Researchers also think that Danish women may be happier than men because women overall have better skills for coping with loss and enjoy stronger social networks. Male or female, we can all aim for those strengths.

- Retired Danish women also have more security, choices, and financial control of their lives than most people in the world. The Melbourne Mercer Global Pension Index (MMGPI) ranked Denmark's pension program first of the twenty-five studied. For everyone not retiring in Denmark, planning well for retirement may be an important consideration for happiness longevity.

# Say What

THE ENGLISH LANGUAGE IS RICH WITH PHRASES TO EXPRESS being happy: You can be "tickled pink," "pleased as punch," and enjoy "a whale of a good time." Many of the phrases about happiness have to do with being "up:"

- Walking on air

- Jumping for joy

- On cloud nine

- As high as a kite,

- High spirits

- On top of the world

- In seventh heaven

- Over the moon

The phrase "over the moon" to express joy goes back hundreds of years. Charles Molloy wrote in his 1718 comedy *The Coquet or The English Chevalier,* "Tis he! I know him now: I shall jump over the Moon for Joy!"

Later in the eighteenth century, "the cow jumped over the moon" in the Mother Goose nursery rhyme that begins "Hey, diddle, diddle, the cat and the fiddle."

Being unhappy is more associated with down—downhearted, down in the mouth, and down in the dumps.

Up, up, and away!

# Color Me Happy

WHICH COLORS MAKE YOU HAPPY? ONE SCHOOL OF thought in color psychology is that blue is for relaxation and calm, red is for passion and energy, purple is luxury, and green is the color of happiness, because it connotes nature and escape.

Maybe you have different associations.

For many, yellow is the hue to pick for a happiness pick-me-up. Some say that the bright color, suggesting sunshine, is the cheeriest color, perking up optimism and joy.

Yellow is the first color to be noticed against a dark background, and it's used to get attention. Taxicabs and the iconic smiley face are yellow.

In Chinese culture, red is often associated with good fortune and happiness, so many gates are painted red.

Take a look at the colors you wear, the colors in the rooms of your home, the colors that dominate your work area. Do they have happy associations for you? Could they help others feel better? What could you change visually that would stimulate smiles or invite a sense of peace and well-being?

# Laughter as Medicine

*It has always seemed to me that hearty laughter is a good way to jog internally without having to go outdoors.*

—Norman Cousins

DECADES AGO, FROM HIS SICK BED, NORMAN COUSINS proved the adage "Laughter is the best medicine." Really! He found that ten minutes of laughter from watching funny TV could help him sleep and heal, and be positive enough to deal with pain.

Research has since shown that laughter not only boosts the immune system and prevents illness, but it can also speed up the healing process. One study revealed that people who had a heart attack were three times as likely to have a second one if they didn't laugh daily, compared to those heart attack survivors who chuckled each day.

Laughter can also dramatically increase one's threshold for pain. Another study showed that even hearing laughter can help some people change body posture and mood for the better.

RXLaughter, a nonprofit organization formed to help children with serious medical problems, uses comedy clips, humor therapy, and laughter therapy. They found that even when humor doesn't make the children laugh out loud, it can help them deal with pain, anxiety, and healing.

# Worry

*Happy is the man who has broken the chains which hurt the mind, and has given up worrying once and for all.*

—Ovid

A MODERN HUMAN IN THE WESTERN WORLD GIVING UP worrying? Fat chance. Billions of dollars are spent for advertising and branding to play into our worries: worries that we and our loved ones aren't thin enough, smart enough, safe enough, healthy enough, good enough, or rich enough. Or, for that matter, happy enough.

Of course, we could refuse to buy in, and ask instead:

- Whose standards are we suffering from?

- What if all is as it should be at this moment?

- Or what if you let go and trust that a higher being will take care of everything?

- Or what if you let go, realizing that nobody has control?

...And you just decide to laugh?

# CHO

THE COAL MINERS, FACTORY WORKERS, AND FARMERS OF the last century probably would have been amazed if anyone had asked them to take a survey about what would make them feel better at work. Certainly, in the century before that, the contemporaries of Charles Dickens would have been boggled if they had been asked to rate their "life satisfaction" by their employers. Today, however, these questions are issues that have generated a new job title: the Chief Happiness Officer, or CHO.

Now, some companies have CHOs who advise the CEOs and CFOs about how to provide more smiles and laughter in the workplace.

For some companies, the motivation behind the position is a genuine interest in their employees' well-being. For others, it's an experimental pathway to more profits. Some studies show that happy employees are more productive and have fewer sick days and lower absenteeism rates.

People used to question whether success was a reliable road to happiness. Now, the question has been turned around, as people investigate whether happiness is actually the path to success.

# JGF

DO AN INTERNET SEARCH FOR "JOLLY GOOD FELLOW," AND you may learn that the multi-billion-dollar company Google has a key staff position with that job title. What started as an inside joke soon became real, and now it's starting to affect the outer world.

The fellow who helms the post, Chade-Meng Tan, was originally a key engineer in developing Google's mobile search service. Now, as Google's JGF, Tan focuses on a different search—people's search for happiness and calm. He claims his job description is "Enlighten minds, open hearts, create world peace."

With a mandate like that, it might be hard to know where to begin, but Tan has built a path that includes meditation, compassion, mindfulness, and humor. In the process, he created SIY (Search Inside Yourself), a company program and best-selling book to introduce his techniques to the rest of the world.

Are you prepared to take on the role of Jolly Good Fellow for your family, reading group, or team at work?

# Your

Not fleeting happiness for the quick indulgence and pleasures that are often based on cravings. Cravings for attention and external affirmations, or cravings from addictions, only escalate. As soon as cravings are filled at one level, you crave more.

Not the illusory happiness of distraction from your own anxieties, disappointments, and shortcomings. Whether it's electronic screen time (television, smartphones, etc.) or gossip or manufactured problems ("my new chair can't be delivered until Saturday"), when you aren't focusing on your distractions, the real problems are still there and so are your fears, resentments, and angers, whether warranted or not.

Not the ignorant happiness based on ignoring unhappiness, denying any serious problems, and underestimating external factors. That does not encourage solutions or growth that could mean a more lasting happiness.

Try, instead, your happiness in being the best "You," and forgiving that your best is still a work in progress.

# Forgive

*Wink at small faults; remember thou hast great ones.*

—Benjamin Franklin

ONE OF THE GREATEST POWERS OF GIVING IS—FORGIVING.
Forgive yourself. Forgive others. And ask to be forgiven.

How can we ever hope nations will stop warring, if we choose as individuals to hug anger instead of love?

Too much of human misery is clinging to what is wrong, or perceived to be wrong, without aiming and working for a larger "right."

Even if we know we are right and find others to agree, are we still a victim of being wronged instead of a strong and gracious agent for good change?

Professor Luskin at the Stanford University Forgiveness Project says forgiveness can help you be a hero instead of a victim. Sometimes it is a slow process, and may require others to help, but the positive results can be worth the effort and wait.

Happiness literature continually includes "forgiveness" as one of the most powerful components of a happier and healthier life.

Go for it! And let the "it" be "give."

Go For Give. Go forgive!

For Happiness.

# HEA

HEA is Internet shorthand and an acronym for "Happily Ever After," as in the classic fairytale ending, "...and they lived happily ever after." We want our lives and our fiction to let all the good guys have all the good stuff.

When George Bernard Shaw wrote *Pygmalion*, he didn't HEA the ending, and his readers were upset. Despite pressures, he wouldn't change the ending, but subsequent producers did.

*My Fair Lady*, the movie and stage musical based on Shaw's work, was modified to have an HEA ending. Both versions were very successful.

The power of HEA worked.

What would HEA be for the story of your life? What will you do today to head in that direction?

# Encore

WHEN A FRIEND OF HERS HAD CANCER, AWARD-WINNING cabaret singer Lauren Fox put together two hours of happy music for her. "Music has the power to transport us," Fox said. "Singing is what I do for my own happiness, and bringing music to others makes me the happiest."

What five songs make you the happiest?

1. _____

2. _____

3. _____

4. _____

5. _____

Make sure that they are just a push button away, and keep adding to the mix. Sing them by yourself—in the stress of traffic, in the shower, while on a walk. Share them with others.

Listen, sing, and share the music that makes you happy!

# Happy Songs

Sing it, baby!

Here are the top twenty "happy" songs in the English language, according to Billboard. The songs with "happy" or "happiness" in the title are ranked by their duration and position on the charts:

"Happy Together," The Turtles
"Don't Worry, Be Happy," Bobby McFerrin
"The Happy Organ," Dave "Baby" Cortez
"My Happiness," Connie Francis
"If You Wanna Be Happy," Jimmy Soul
"You've Made Me So Very Happy," Blood, Sweat & Tears
"Love Can Make You Happy," Mercy
"Happy Days," Pratt & McClain with Brother Love
"Happy Birthday, Sweet Sixteen," Neil Sedaka
"Sha-La-La (Make Me Happy)," Al Green
"Hotel Happiness," Brook Benton
"Oh Happy Day," The Edwin Hawkins Singers
"Happy," Ashanti
"If It Makes You Happy," Sheryl Crow
"Shiny Happy People," R.E.M.
"My Happy Ending," Avril Lavigne
"Happy," Pharrell Williams
"Happy-Go-Lucky Me," Paul Evans

"The Happiest Girl in the Whole U.S.A.," Donna Fargo
"Oh, How Happy," Shades of Blue

These songs are chosen by title, not by lyrics. Some are actually sad. A global survey, though, concluded that some sad music can help people feel better. They may feel empathy or catharsis (which helps regulate emotions). Or they may drift off, glad the problems in the song aren't theirs.

And happy music—well you know how you feel.

Happy listening!

# Move

Jump, dance, and wave your arms.

You've heard it before: Exercise can improve your mood, well-being, and sleep. It can even reduce anxiety, while sending oxygen to the brain and body and releasing endorphins—all ingredients for feeling happy.

Nevertheless, many of us spend most of our awake time sitting—reading, watching TV, working, or playing video games. Next time you find yourself cemented in sedentariness, give movement a try. It's amazing how just getting out of the coach-potato position and doing some silly moves can move your spirit, too.

From schlump to jump, you can pump yourself from deflation toward a bit of elation. Many researchers say that getting cardio exercise for even a few minutes can help your health and well-being, in both the short and long term. The National Health Population Survey gathered data about exercise over a fourteen-year period, and their analysis showed that the long-term effects of physical activity can reduce unhappiness even two and four years after the sweat has dried.

So go for it (with your doctor's approval, of course).

Don't miss a chance to jump for joy!

# Greenercise—Outdoor Ups!

Next time you want to exercise, you might want to think green and head outside to a favorite park instead of to the gym. There's evidence that it could be better for you.

Several different groups of researchers have concluded that exercising outdoors can have greater physical and mental impact than exercising inside, so it could better support your happiness.

In terms of feelings of well-being, exercise in a natural environment significantly beats exercise between walls and beneath ceilings. The type of outdoor exercise—walking, sailing, gardening, or biking—didn't matter. Walking outdoors in nature also beat walking outdoors in an urban area. Green environments were found to improve both mood and levels of self-esteem.

The really good news? You're likely to see results in a very short time. The studies showed it takes only five minutes of outdoor exercise for some positive impact to kick in.

# Nothing

SO MUCH OF CONTEMPORARY LIFE IS ABOUT THINGS AND happiness. Here are some thoughts about "no-thing" that might relate to happiness.

*Nothing to do... Nothing to do... What a happy thought!*

—Winnie the Pooh

*There is nothing either good or bad, but thinking makes it so.*

—William Shakespeare, *Hamlet*

*The world is a dangerous place, not because of those who do evil, but because of those who look on and do nothing.*

—Albert Einstein

*I think it would be amazing if I would get to play beautiful parts and win Oscars, but that would all mean nothing if my parents and friends weren't there with me. What is success when you don't have anybody to love? No, I'd rather be happily married.*

—Emma Watson

*Life is either a daring adventure or nothing at all.*

—Helen Keller

*Nothing in life is to be feared, it is only to be understood.*

—Marie Curie

These quotes were culled from "Random Quotes," a collection of many hundreds of diverse quotes gathered over the last seven years by nineteen-year-old Analee Rose Dorff. Tolstoy gathered his aphorisms for decades before he published *A Calendar of Wisdom,* so she has some time—to do "nothing."

# I Want

A CHILD SAID TO A SAGE, "I WANT HAPPINESS."

The sage answered, "Get rid of the 'I,' that's just your ego. It keeps you separated from others and is an illusion. It makes you selfish and needy and dissatisfied, so you suffer. Ego is a sieve that wants constant feeding. So get rid of the 'I.'"

The sage continued, "Now get rid of the 'want.' Desiring things takes away from enjoying what you have and focuses on expectations that may not be fulfilling. It implies you will be happy, if something else—if you have more fame, money, success, friends. It makes you wait and compare.

"If you take away the 'I' and the 'want' of 'I want Happiness,' what is left?" the sage asked.

"Happiness," the child said.

And smiled.

Shorter versions of the "I Want Happiness" story have floated around for a long time, sometimes falsely attributed to Buddha.

What's your version?

# FoMO

FoMO is an acronym for "Fear of Missing Out."

We live in a time of abundance including an abundance of options. Whether it's deciding what event to go to on a weekend, what entree to order, whom to spend the day with, or what shore excursion to select on a cruise, FoMO causes some people to mar their own happiness. Whatever options they choose, they worry they are missing something better.

With social media and instant communications, we can be more aware than ever of what other people are doing. If we are afraid that they are choosing better than us, instead of happy that they are happy, then *any* piece of the proverbial pie can create indigestion, instead of satisfaction.

Being stressed about FoMO and making choices between great options is truly a "First-World Problem." How fortunate we are to have choices! Most people in history and on the planet today have never had such a plentitude of possibilities.

Instead of FoMO standing for "Fear of Missing Out," wouldn't it be great if the FoMO mindset was the "Fun of Many Opportunities"?

Enjoy your choice—it's yours!

# If

*If—*

*If you can keep your head when all about you*
      *Are losing theirs and blaming it on you;*
*If you can trust yourself when all men doubt you,*
      *But make allowance for their doubting too;*
*If you can wait and not be tired by waiting,*
      *Or being lied about, don't deal in lies,*
*Or being hated, don't give way to hating,*
      *And yet don't look too good, nor talk too wise:*

*If you can dream, and not make dreams your master;*
      *If you can think, and not make thoughts your aim;*
*If you can meet with Triumph and Disaster*
      *And treat those two imposters just the same;*
*If you can bear to hear the truth you've spoken*
      *Twisted by knaves to make a trap for fools,*
*Or watch the things you gave your life to, broken,*
      *And stoop and build 'em up with worn-out tools;*

*If you can make one heap of all your winnings*
      *And risk it on one turn of pitch-and-toss,*
*And lose, and start again at your beginnings*
      *And never breathe a word about your loss;*
*If you can force your heart and nerve and sinew*
      *To serve your turn long after they are gone,*

*And so hold on when there is nothing in you*
    *Except the Will which says to them: "Hold on!"*

*If you can talk with crowds and keep your virtue,*
    *Or walk with Kings, nor lose the common touch,*
*If neither foes nor loving friends can hurt you,*
    *If all men count with you, but none too much;*
*If you can fill the unforgiving minute*
    *With sixty seconds' worth of distance run,*
*Yours is the Earth and everything that's in it,*
    *And—which is more—you'll be a Man, my son!*
                                    —Rudyard Kipling

RUDYARD KIPLING'S POEM "IF—," WRITTEN IN 1895, WAS voted Britain's favorite poem in 1995, according to a BBC opinion poll. It proposes many ways to live with both engagement and detachment for a full life. Which couplets speak to you as a way to be happier? What lessons do you draw from them?

# Serenity Prayer

*God grant me the serenity*
*to accept the things I cannot change;*
*courage to change the things I can;*
*and wisdom to know the difference.*
*Living one day at a time;*
*enjoying one moment at a time;*
*accepting hardships as the pathway to peace;*
*taking, as He did, this sinful world*
*as it is, not as I would have it;*
*trusting that He will make all things right*
*if I surrender to His Will;*
*that I may be reasonably happy in this life*
*and supremely happy with Him*
*forever in the next.*
*Amen.*

—Reinhold Niebuhr

THE SERENITY PRAYER WAS WRITTEN BY THEOLOGIAN
Dr. Reinhold Niebuhr, an American Protestant, though its
key message is found centuries earlier in other cultures, too.

The first four lines are well known to many who
participate in Alcoholics Anonymous (AA) and other
twelve-step groups. During World War II, the first stanza
of the Serenity Prayer was printed by AA and the National
Council of Churches, and it was handed out worldwide:

*What can't you change?*
*What can you change?*
*What can't you change that you want to accept*
   *or forgive?*
*What can you change that you will try to change?*

# Make Your Day

LIKE OTHER ANIMALS, HUMANS ARE GEARED TO PAY attention to what is wrong, to scout for danger. That is part of primal survival. But unlike most animals, humans can also direct their thoughts to happier things than fear and anxiety when real danger is not imminent. In today's modern world, that seems essential to the quality of survival.

Gather the positive. Notice beauty. Collect kindness. Use all your senses to appreciate the world around you: See, smell, touch, taste, and hear the elements that make you feel better.

Take extra moments to let yourself savor those positive nuggets. Pain and ugliness are real, but can you help the wonders of the world outweigh the worries in your sphere?

Notice what makes others happier. A smile. An offer to help. Just listening. Sharing your mints. Giving a genuine compliment.

Have you ever stopped on a busy corner just to listen and smell, or to make eye contact and smile at someone?

And don't forget to laugh!

# Enjoy Now...

*What a wonderful life I've had! I only wish I had
realized it sooner.*

—Colette

MANY PEOPLE LOOK BACK AND THINK THINGS WERE BETTER
in the past—"the good ole days." Some think that all society
and culture were somehow different, somehow better "back
then." Other times, "the good ole days" are more personal—
the fun times had in days gone by (even if you didn't see
them as good at the time).

The truth is, if you live long enough, today could be
among the "good ole days" you look back on through your
rear-view mirror. Realize it now, and enjoy what you have.

Sometimes we look at photos of our younger selves,
surprised by how good we looked compared to now. In
the same way, today's image could be beautiful to us in the
future, when we look back and see ourselves as we are now.

Why wait? Appreciate the beauties you have now.
Enjoy what is wonderful now.

# The 3 Ings

WHEN HE TEACHES POSITIVE PSYCHOLOGY, DR. STEVE
Taylor tells his students that there are three pathways to
happiness: Doing, Thinking, and Being. Here are some of
the kinds of activities that can go in each category.

## DOING

Help others
Exercise and eat well
Act on goals
Learn and create
Sleep
Head into nature
Hang out with positive people

## BEING

Tap into the spiritual
Withdraw from the outer world of stimuli
Meditate
Empty your mind and find the quiet within
Find your inner natural happiness

## THINKING

Guide thinking toward the positive instead of the
negative

Rewrite your negative scripts
Read uplifting books
Develop a mindset of gratitude
Notice your thoughts
Talk to positive thinkers

IN HIS BOOK, *SPONTANEOUS HAPPINESS*, DR. ANDREW WEIL suggests three portals for happiness:

Caring for the Body
Caring for the Mind
Caring for the Spirit, and engaging in a Secular Spirituality

When practiced together, he says, the threesome forms a path to a state of happiness that can be maintained as a kind of "emotional sea level."

Here is a list of ten practices Dr. Weil believes will help anyone who follows them:

Exercise
Follow an anti-inflammatory diet
Take fish oil and vitamin D
Take depression-specific herbs
Do breathing exercises
Try cognitive behavioral therapy (CBT)
Laugh
Limit media exposure
Forgive
Practice gratitude

# Inertia

WE READ ALL THESE THINGS ABOUT HAPPINESS AND THINK, "Maybe I should try that." But will we actually change direction or velocity and do something different?

Going back a few hundred years, scientifically, inertia is part of Isaac Newton's First Law of Motion. He described it in his *Philosophiæ Naturalis Principia Mathematica* as "The *vis insita*, or innate force of matter, is a power of resisting by which every body, as much as in it lies, endeavours to preserve its present state, whether it be of rest or of moving uniformly forward in a straight line."

Put in more modern language: a body at rest tends to stay at rest, and a body in motion tends to stay in motion in the same direction. Inertia is the resistance of a physical object to change.

How will you, as a physical object, overcome your own inertia? Unlike inanimate objects, we can move ourselves and overcome inertia.

How can you change your *vis insita* to do new things for your happiness?

What in this book do you want to try?

May you overcome your inertia for moments of elation and achieve the momentum for lasting happiness!

# Thanks, aka Acknowledgments

EVERY DAY I WORKED ON THIS BOOK, I WAS HAPPY AND thankful, and I *still* am! Gratitude to editor Chris Barsanti at Sterling Publishing and Infopreneur Andrea Rotondo for thinking of me for the project. Thanks also to copy editor Beth Gruber for vetting commas and content, and to all the folks at Sterling who made the book possible.

Thanks warmly to all the people who have taught me about happiness and brought so much of it into my world, starting with my dear parents, Ross and Ann Sonne, and including all the multitudinous, splendiferous rest of you— family and friends—in niches around the earth. (I hope you know who you are, because I have taken the time to thank you before in person!)

While writing the book, I tested some of the happiness ideas about nature, travel, meditation, and people on an *Uncruise*, while island hopping in Hawaii. Thanks to all the passengers and crew who shared the delights with me, and especially Wellness coach Paul, and the three-generation Traber Family, whose eight-year-old Mollie reminded me of the sheer joy of laughing uncontrollably.

Additional thanks to those who helped with the book, but weren't mentioned in the text...until now: Jamey Cohen, Shari Cohen, Sri Hari, Paul and Libby Kaufman, Bonnie Olsen, James Sonne, Ilona Scott, and Kathy Spielman.

Appreciation goes also to all those who are working to understand, to share, and to spread happiness as a kindness, not a commodity, and to all those sharing their research and insights.

And, of course, invaluable thanks go to the guy who adds to my happiness every day, my husband, Victor. We try to make each other's books and lives better, and he succeeds lovingly. I am grateful!

# About the Writer

WHEN SHE WAS TWO YEARS OLD, LISA T.E. SONNE WOULD hug everybody who came to the door, from her grandmother to the postman. As a teenager, she decided to try to live up to her last name, which means "soul" and "sun," and aim to give light and warmth to others. She loves sharing inspiring stories and beauty through her award-winning work in writing, photography, and television.

In her travels on the seven continents and many seas of the world, Sonne has seen a great gamut of despair and delight. She and her husband decided to be Possibilitators—people who make things possible. After helping launch *space.com*, they founded the nonprofit Charity Checks (www.CharityChecks.us) to usher in the concept of giving others the "Joy of Giving." Instead of gift cards to buy consumer goods, "Giving Certificates" let the recipients choose good causes, donate the funds to them, and feel the happiness of giving.

When asked to write in "marital status" on forms, she and her husband both put "happy."

Sonne's other books include: *Everything 101: A Complete Education in a Snap*, *Buddha Meditations: The Art of Letting Go*, and *My Adventures: A Traveler's Journal*.

Her website is www.LisaSonne.com